I0052150

Copyright © 2018 by Naomi Johnson

All rights reserved. This book or any portion thereof may not be reproduced or used in any manner whatsoever without the express written permission of the publisher except for the use of brief quotations in a book review or scholarly journal.

First Edition: 2015
Second Edition: 2018

ISBN 978-0-9568055-3-9

TheProfile.Company, Technopole, Kingston Crescent, Portsmouth, PO2 8FA

Cover Design by Naomi Johnson

Photo of Naomi Johnson by
Janette Edmonds

www.TheProfile.Company

Dedication

To those who believe with dedication
and stay the course

TABLE OF CONTENTS

Foreword 7

1. Introduction 9

2. Using LinkedIn 55

3. Strategy 69

4. How to Use This Book 87

A WARNING 88

5. Profile Basics...................91

6. Intermediate.................. 121

7. Advanced 173

Foreword

There are many books on how to use LinkedIn, but in my opinion, they tend to be a bit one-dimensional. In this book, Naomi takes a unique perspective in showing how to bring a LinkedIn profile to life, how to develop a rapport with a profile visitor, and how to make your profile a vital part of your marketing mix to build your sales funnel.

I met Naomi in 2014 while working on a webcast about making a return on investment from social selling and how to use LinkedIn to achieve this. The team's marketing efforts attracted an audience of 1200, proving that this is a hot topic for many.

During our work together, we discussed many aspects of social selling, including LinkedIn and the importance of profiles. When I heard Naomi had set up a company and written a book solely focused on writing LinkedIn profiles, I was pleased. A LinkedIn profile is perhaps the most vital part of a social selling strategy as all proactive and active behaviour comes back to the questions 'Who are you? What's special about you? Why do I want to work with you?' A LinkedIn profile needs to answer these—and quickly too—something most people writing their profiles can't easily achieve.

In this book, Naomi maps out how to create a profile that complements a prospect's buying cycle and how to take full advantage of each field available on the profile and match this with your existing marketing activities, sales funnel, and social selling strategy.

Naomi's book provides coaching and a programmatic approach to support the proactive LinkedIn beginner and the power user. If you are one of those people who want to use LinkedIn as a tool to support a social selling initiative, acquire leads, meet your quota, and gain a competitive advantage, this is for you.

About Tim Hughes

Tim Hughes is a pioneer and innovator in the area of social selling. After being involved in the rollout of social selling at Oracle across some 2000 people, he came up with his five-pillar methodology to enable small and large companies to implement social selling for competitive advantage. He is the co-founder of the social selling community website SocialSalesLounge.com, which offers advice and coaching to companies that want their salespeople to exceed their quotas and do it quick.

1. Introduction

In this short book, I am going to share with you the advice I've given and the stories I've told countless others while working with an international LinkedIn training provider and subsequently within my own company, writing LinkedIn Profiles for business people.

In talking with hundreds of sales professionals, HR managers, and business owners, I have realised that the biggest question people have about LinkedIn is what to put on their profile.

And rightly so.

LinkedIn is your window to the world and, in many cases, the first impression you give. In the last 20 years, since the birth of the Internet, we've seen a dramatic change in the way people buy products and services. Research conducted by LinkedIn and Altermeir in 2012 has proven that at least 57% of a person's decision to buy is now made online before contact is made with a sales representative. In the fast-moving consumer goods industry, this number can range anywhere between 57-100%.

As you probably know from reflecting on your behaviour, today we are more likely to research, read reviews and purchase online, than to spend hours with a sales assistant asking questions, or walking into a shop.

Fundamentally, how people buy has changed.

For businesses this has created many advantages, allowing them to reduce overheads and cut the cost of winning new sales.

For fast moving consumer goods (FMCG), a sale can now be achieved entirely online with no human contact required at all. A buyer is confident to make their own choices and take the risk they may get it wrong.

For service-based businesses who are time-sensitive and resource-poor, the ability to cultivate our marketing place and only speak to prospects when they are ready to buy dramatically reduces the cost of each new sale and ability to build a profitable business.

Unlike the FMCG industry though, service-based businesses do need to spend time with their customers before they purchase, and for a good reason. Before accepting the sale, they need to first make sure they can actually help.

A time-sensitive business will never achieve 100% of a buying decision online like other industries. Yet that isn't to say we can't build our online content and resources to bring a prospect as close to purchasing as possible, and have those who aren't our ideal prospect opt of our sales funnel, saving us a great deal of time.

Why LinkedIn

Of all the social media platforms LinkedIn is by far the strongest and most powerful when it comes to business, whether that be for winning your customers, sourcing suppliers or making a career move.

With 550 million members across the globe and counting, LinkedIn makes it easy to find decision-makers and new connections within a few clicks.

It has also become an integral place for professionals to find one another. It is now natural for people to research prospective clients and suppliers on the platform before a meeting. In fact, with Microsoft Dynamics, this is even more likely since the calendar function now includes the LinkedIn profile of the person we are meeting with the appointment reminder itself.

Publishing the right content and making the right impression is imperative. Good information will allow both parties to come to the meeting informed, and well crafted information that assists prospects in their buying decision will advance the conversation and dramatically improve the chances of the prospect buying from us since they will have already have assessed how suitable we are for them, before they reached out to speak to us.

Our LinkedIn profiles are an important part of our personal brand as not only do people look to find us on LinkedIn, but our profiles also come up in any name-based search on Google.

A LinkedIn profile forms our personal brand and communicates a powerful impression of whom we are.

By crafting it carefully, we can easily position ourselves as an expert and authority figure within our industry and create unlimited opportunities.

It simply comes down to what we want and how we pitch it.

You get what you pitch for and you're always pitching – Daniel Priestley

Your Personal Brand is Everything

In this new age, your personal brand is your greatest asset and something that requires time to develop. You might think that you're just in a job or just selling this product, but actually you're selling yourself, as today people buy people. Succeeding within our career, whether that is as an employed person or as a self-employed person, comes down to our ability to sell ourselves, and the value we can bring to an organisation.

We are no longer just selling something; we are selling ourselves. Buyers no longer want to buy from faceless organisations, but rather from the people within them and what they stand for. There is a growing sense of wanting to be part of something greater than ourselves, and business being a simple transaction.

People want to buy from people they know, like and trust. Or better yet, people they aspire to be like.

Before now we didn't have this option. We had to buy from big, faceless organisations whether we agreed with their ethics and motivations or not. They held the large marketing budgets and power within industries that blocked smaller companies from getting ahead.

However social media has levelled the playing field, transforming the business world and making it possible for an individual to become a global sensation overnight without leaving their bedroom.

Barriers to entry have crumbled, and more and more people can follow their passion and work when they choose, for whom they choose, and from where they choose.

As an organisation, there is a growing need to open the doors and welcome people in, to be transparent and add value to our marketplace.

And to introduce our marketplace to our people.

For many companies, the idea of exposing their greatest asset – the talented people who work for them – is terrifying, especially as LinkedIn is also known as a recruitment platform.

However, a balance must be found where individuals can develop their personal brand in line with the company in such a way that they are able to win new business for the company without the company losing their best people.

Ultimately this will come down to company culture and many other aspects of human resource management, but the need to accomplish this is great.

As we have said, people buy from people. People they know like and trust. And therefore organisations can no longer afford to hide their people. They must bring their talent to the forefront and allow their prospects and customers to get to know their staff while controlling the message, because if they don't, LinkedIn is doing it for them anyway.

Brand-conscious organisations know that the profile of each member of their staff is contributing to their overall company image, perhaps more powerfully than any other marketing material they produce.

They know that the majority of their staff are on LinkedIn and that their profiles are connected to the company's LinkedIn page. Therefore any prospect or customer can quickly and easily find and view the profiles of their staff, and each contributes to the impression they are forming of the company, its people and their ability to deliver.

At this point in time, a profile filled out like a CV will appear normal and nothing more will be expected. However, blank or incomplete profiles will be considered "slightly lacking," but as we progress, and more companies begin to understand the importance of positioning their staff as experts within their industry as an asset, poorly crafted profiles will begin to lose sales.

It will be the companies that understand how people buy and takes advantage of the value each member of their team contributes towards a positive buying decision that will excel. Doing this now, and being first within your industry to do so, will make you stand out from the crowd.

A LinkedIn profile can build loyalty with existing clients or new ones.

If we want to get ahead and take full advantage of the times we find ourselves in, we'd do well to focus our attention on creating our personal brand and becoming someone people want to buy from, whether this is as an Expert or Trusted Advisor within our industry, or as a personality within our organisation.

Our careers and the opportunities we create come down to how willing we are to position ourselves within our marketplace and get found.

Everything Comes Back to the Profile

Your LinkedIn profile is a powerful piece of the free real estate that is uniquely positioned among all the people that know, like, and trust you. By connecting with people you already know, and new people you meet, you gain exposure to every person your connection knows. With this multiplier effect, the ability to get your message out into the world and in front of the right people is endless.

But with everything you do on LinkedIn to build your network and your influence, everything hangs on your profile.

Your success on LinkedIn will depend on how well you pitch your business and draw your prospect into your sales funnel.

When it comes to using LinkedIn, there are three potential strategies you might use:

1. **Proactive**: Identifying exactly whom you wish to be connected with, and directly seeking out a relationship with them

2. **Active**: Building up awareness by increasing your connections, contributing to discussions, publishing content and sharing status updates

3. **Passive**: Pitching your services, your experience, and ethos on your LinkedIn profile with a strong call-to-action

Each of these strategies will gain you vital exposure to your message. However, with each activity, your profile is always the most prominent and important piece. Whether you comment on someone's status, join a discussion, send a connect request, share a picture, publish content, or ask to be introduced to someone, everything comes back to your profile.

Active   **Proactive**

Passive

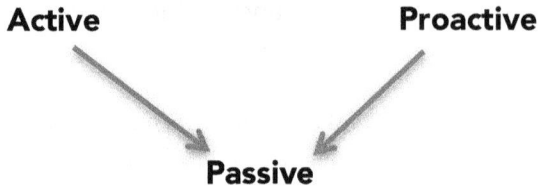

As we navigate around the platform sowing into your network, we naturally become curious about people and want to find out more. We come to a profile wanting to learn more about a person, and ready to read their profile.

With only an active interest and curiosity, they will still be asking 'how are you relevant to me?' People are time sensitive and won't read information that isn't relevant or timely for them. This is why CV based LinkedIn profiles with lots of big words generally turn people off. If the person isn't in recruitment, they aren't interested. People come to your profile wanting to connect with you, a person, and therefore your profile needs to give them that. A connection.

Your profile visitor needs to be able to learn about you and feel like they've 'met you.' Some of the most powerful words you can use on your profile include 'I believe,' 'In my opinion,' 'Personally,' and 'In my experience' since this gives us an insight into a person and their motivation.

When someone arrives at your profile they need to quickly understand the context of the conversation they are about to have with you should they read on. Since people are always asking 'is this relevant to me' you need to be telling them.

With all your activities on the platform, your objective needs to create curiosity, so people visit your profile. Your profile needs to pitch your services clearly and tell prospects what to do next if they want to find out more.

Therefore your proactive and active strategies should always have a consistency about them and targeted messaging. For example, if you are promoting yourself as a mortgage expert, make sure you share valuable content about mortgages. Switching content and sharing things about leadership will only confuse your audience and dilute the impact of your brand presence.

With so much information available these days and our audience overloaded with content, we need to remain on point and quickly convey our purpose.

The Right Pigeonhole

As human beings, we are programmed to stereotype and pigeonhole within a matter of seconds, as a way of filtering the information we are continually bombarded with every day. It's a natural part of life. However, since the Internet began, we have become even faster at filtering and dismissing what isn't relevant to us. As a result, if a LinkedIn profile doesn't quickly pique interest and appear relevant, we move on without a second thought.

Therefore, our profile has to show what we do, how we do it and the value we offer quickly. We must write in such a way that our prospects can quickly grasp it and become curious. We need to meet our prospect where they are in their buying cycle and provide engaging information that adds value and leads them to want to spend time with us.

If we fail to provide this information, our prospects will be quick to move on to our competitor who is providing this information.

Further, if we fail to position ourselves correctly, we could find that potential referral partners are either disengaged or referring us to the wrong opportunities. Whatever the case, once an impression is made it is hard to change, so getting it right the first time is important.

Research by Nottingham University have found that we make a first impression about someone within 0.3 seconds, and if the impression is negative, it will take up to eighteen half-hour meetings to reverse this impression.

EXAMPLE: Changing Careers

Example

A few weeks ago, I spoke to a business consultant who, a year before, decided to pursue an acting career. With a friend's help, she staged a few acting scenes, filmed them, and made a showreel. As many acting agents now use LinkedIn, she put the showreel on her LinkedIn profile. Her clients were aware of her brave step into a new career and respected her greatly for it. However, there was just one problem. While those who already knew her heard the real story behind what she was doing and why, those coming to her LinkedIn profile and learning about her for the first time did not know she was first a business consultant, and a credible one.

On her profile, she listed her acting career above her business career. Chronologically this was correct, but for an onlooker, it seemed she was first an actress and second a business consultant. In fact, having watched her showreel first, I had difficulty finding her 'believable' when watching her business video. The order of her content and the absence of her story in summary made me pigeonhole her incorrectly, and in talking to her, I found it hard to get past.

It took 20 minutes of talking to her to let go of this impression and correctly position her in my mind as a successful businesswoman.

Time is not a luxury most of us have with people, especially when they are browsing profiles or dealing with incoming messages.

For this client, while her new venture was working for her face-to-face, it wasn't working for her online. To overcome this, she needed to rearrange her content and tell her story in her summary.

Ensuring that people pigeonhole us correctly and that we end up in the right one, is our sole responsibility, and no one else's.

We achieve it by providing the right information, in the right way. If you are finding that people don't take you seriously or treat you in the way you want, take the time to reflect on how you present yourself, and how you feel about yourself. All of these things are contributing to your brand image and how people engage with you.

Our LinkedIn profile and how we present ourselves is our opportunity, each and every day, to direct.

Everyday we have an incredible opportunity to change the world around us, and how we are invited into new worlds. Ultimately, people will only ever respond to the information we provide.

A good analogy of this would be how I treat different trousers in my wardrobe. The ones I buy for £6 get worn out very quickly as I'll use them for gardening and hiking, whereas the ones I buy for £50 only get worn for work and special occasions. How I interact with each is dictated by how much I spent on them and how much I value them, and little to do with actual quality.

Thus, how we present ourselves and how we put ourselves forward, changes the relationships around us.

A well-constructed LinkedIn profile that engages your prospects establishes your value and your expertise, has the potential to position you as an authority in your industry instantly. It can bring you the best assignments and recommendations, at a fee you choose.

A Good Profile is Never About You

A good LinkedIn profile is never about you but rather about your prospect, and the problem that you can solve for them. Our profiles should never boast or show off our credentials, but rather tell our story and highlight our expertise in the context of the problem we are solving.

Your profile is essentially your business pitch and you have 30 seconds to get it right. If it doesn't peak the interest of your prospect, they will simply click away. They don't even have to excuse themselves from the conversation they can simply click away.

On LinkedIn, your prospects don't have to find a polite way to excuse them self from the conversation—they can simply click away!

How People Read LinkedIn Profiles

The first scan is extremely important. No one will immediately jump into reading each sentence and paragraph until they've made a judgement call on whether it is worthy of their time. A poorly formatted profile will have people click away because people will feel that if you can't take the time to present it well, why should they take the time to read it?

Next, we need to set context, so our visitor quickly grasps the conversation we're about to have. Is it leadership, digital marketing, life coaching? They will want to quickly understand so they can make a judgement call on whether to read on. There is only so long that someone will stick around to find out 'what does this person do?'

Once we've set the context and defined what we do, we need to accurately disqualify those who aren't prospects and draw in those that are. We need to speak about the problem we solve so that those who have that problem and are looking for a solution know they are in the right place.

And those who don't know they have a problem and therefore aren't yet looking for our solution sit up and take notice.

Once we have the attention of our prospects we need to position ourselves as an authority worth listening to, and then outline how we can help.

We then need a compelling 'call to action' that enables our prospect to feel comfortable reaching out and start a conversation with us.

The one thing to be aware of is that your LinkedIn profile replicates meeting at a networking event, only it doesn't come with the etiquette of a face-to-face meeting. LinkedIn is way more brutal. If a prospect isn't interested in what you have to say, they will simply click away. At a networking event, they will smile politely, change the conversation or try to get away, making what you say and how even more important.

If your visitor is now interested in what you offer, your profile also needs to answer the logical questions a person will ask next about your services and how you work. Just the same as they would if you were speaking to them in a conversation.

Each paragraph needs to have information that a prospect will find interesting and need to know to want to move forward with you.

A strong call to action will invite a prospect to have a diagnostic with you and to find out more about the extent of their problem and whether you can help. For this, you are asking a person to exchange time and personal information with you. To get to this end point we need to meet the 57% of a buying decision that is now made offline.

Completed correctly our LinkedIn profile is a powerful marketing tool capable of leveraging trust stored up within in our network from years of hard work, and attract the very best business opportunities.

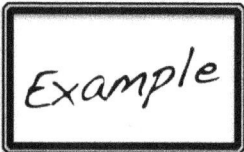

Example

EXAMPLE: The Power of Your Network

When I started my business TheProfile. Company, I announced it on LinkedIn. Within a few hours, I have several invitations to connect, which I responded to asking each person why they wanted to connect.

One person introduced himself told me he was starting a new communications agency and wanted his LinkedIn profile written for himself and his business partner.

It turned out that the only mutual connection we had, and the only way he had discovered my profile was because of our mutual connection who liked my status update. My new client had seen it and become curious about my new company and what I was offering. He visited my profile and was sold. He became my first client.

Word-of-Mouth Recommendations

When we receive word-of-mouth recommendations, it means that we're doing business right—that those who know us are willing to put their business reputation on the line for telling a friend or colleague that we are a reputable provider.

For this reason, word-of-mouth recommendations are one of the most powerful sources of new business.

By referring us, this person is automatically transferring their trust in us to the new business contact, greatly advancing the conversation and our chances of winning the new business available.

If your business relies on word-of-mouth recommendation, LinkedIn is the perfect place for you.

One of the biggest excuses I hear for not using LinkedIn is, 'I don't need LinkedIn—my business relies on word of mouth.'

But what people are failing to recognise is just how influential LinkedIn and how, by getting their profile right, they'd get a lot more word-of-mouth recommendations.

While business referrals are great, they are also a tricky business as they rely heavily on certain steps.

1. The person first has to realise they have a problem that needs solving.

2. They need to mention it in conversation with someone who knows you.

3. The person who knows you need match what you do to the problem they just heard, which means understanding exactly what you do, the problem you solve and the value you provide.

4. They have to be willing to introduce you.

5. They need to be able to pitch your services just right so the person with the problem feels motivated to seek you out, even if it takes a few days or weeks to receive your information.

6. The introducer needs to have your details to hand to be able to pass them

over before they conclude that it's not worth the effort.

7. The prospect must feel comfortable calling you to discuss the problem and confident it is a good use of their time, which there is some likelihood they would invest in your solution.

8. They must understand the extent of their problem and the cost of not solving it to perceive the need to invest in the solution.

9. They need to justify to themselves, and those around them, why hiring you is a necessity.

If any of these steps is missed, you'll never know if a word of mouth recommendation was given. It takes successfully navigating each of these steps to produce a new business lead.

LinkedIn solves them all.

If network understands the problem you solve and the value you provide, they will recognise the problem in others and recommend you – whether they actually know you or not. People love to help and especially appear knowledgeable. Being able to provide a solution by making a good recommendation is almost addictive. It is something people love to do, so even if someone hasn't met you, but instead know, like and trust you simply from your online presence, they will refer you.

Making an introduction via LinkedIn is easy to do. With just your name they can hand over all your business information and secure the quality recommendation, they intended, creating a great impression of them and for you.

Even standing in a bar a person can quickly assess you and decide whether they want to reach out or not. Once they have clicked 'connect' you, the seller, are now in charge of the buying conversation and can follow up with them.

With your solution pitched well and you invitation to get in touch clear, there is every chance that this recommendation will now turn into a positive opportunity.

Your prospect will come to the first meeting with you, whether face-to-face or over the phone, with a good understanding of what you do, how you do it, and why you do it. If they are showing up for the meeting, it is because they acknowledge they have a pain they are motivated to solve, and they are hoping you will be able to help.

Relying on word-of-mouth also tends to have another nasty drawback. Along with not being able to control the multiple drop-points listed above, there is also the fact that without a clear LinkedIn profile and business pitch, you will have no control over the type of referrals you receive.

When we fail to provide clear information that accurately pitches our business and who it is we want to do business with, we provide no way for a prospect to disqualify themselves from our sales process.

Instead, we'll have referrals approach us for projects that really aren't our speciality or what we want to be doing. Because the person has come to us via recommendation, we feel obligational to help. After all, it is hard to say 'no' to a request to spend time with someone when it has come from a mentor or business colleague that we respect.

However, a good LinkedIn profile should have your referee look at your profile and quickly ascertain that their problem isn't what you fix. Instead, they should be saying 'That's not my problem, this solution isn't for me' and give them the opportunity to walk away from a conversation before it begins. It might sound strange, but in our time-sensitive businesses, we simply don't have time speak to people who will never buy simply because they were referred to us. It is lovely when someone offers you a recommendation, but it doesn't necessarily follow we'll be a perfect match.

In my business, I make it clear I do not write profiles or provide advise for people seeking new jobs. When people refer me, a quick look at my profile will have the person say 'this isn't the right match for me' and move on to another supplier.

There have been times when clients have made speaking to a friend or relative part of the deal of winning their business. In these instances, it is hard to say no, so I do my best providing the right advice, letting them know that it isn't an area I specialise in. It's awkward for both parties.

If we aren't clear within ourselves the type of business we want to take on and neither is our marketplace and those that refer us, we'll likely agree to take on assignments that aren't right for us.

Not only will this remove the enjoyment of our business but it'll put us under enormous strain as we try to fit them in a while attracting those we do want. There is every likelihood too that your client will feel it and feel undervalued, which could impact upon your ability to win new business in the future.

If we do make this client happy, there is also a strong likelihood that they will tell their friends and recommend you. They will think they are doing you a favour, when actually they are clogging your sales funnel with less than ideal clients and branding your business.

What people say about us and how the introduce us, establishes us in our marketplace. So if our clients are getting it wrong, what chance do we have of correcting them and getting known for the business we really want to be winning?

We need to avoid boxing ourselves into the wrong market segment at all costs, and this requires us to manage our message, our pitch and be selective whom we take on.

If we are experiencing lean times, we might want just to accept the job – after all, it is money - but all we'll be doing is setting our self up for a harder time in the future, as we'll just end up attracting more of the same.

The only way to break this cycle is to be willing to turn undesirable prospects away and educate our existing clients and referral partners on what we actually do and the types of clients we want. By updating your profile accurately with a clear pitch, we can begin to take back control.

When we pitch our business well, we begin to receive word-of-mouth recommendations that are the types of assignments we actually want to be doing. We become known for delivering excellence in our field and gain knowledge, insight, and expertise in it, and we become able to command our fees.

Further, if we want to create our dream business and succeed in our vision, we need to learn to say no and focus on gaining the attention of the right type of prospects.

Leveraging Word-of-Mouth Recommendations

As they say, 'It's not what you know but who you know!' In the old days, this statement referred to nepotism, where the best jobs and opportunities were reserved for those within our close family network or friendship groups.

Today though, this has changed, and social mobility is entirely of our own making. By building relationships, adding value and managing our reputation we can advance through life without limitation.

We can do this by remembering that people buy from people; people they know, like and trust.

> *People buy from people, and they buy from people they know, like, and trust.*

Therefore if we want to be recognised for what we do, if we want to be introduced to the best opportunities, we simply have to become someone that people want to buy from.

When an introduction is given, there is a transfer of trust from the person introducing to the person considering working with you. This transfer of trust is often the foundation for a good working relationship and why you'll win the contract in the first place.

If you want to gain entry into any industry or have an audience with an influential or hard-to-access person, all you need to do is ask for an introduction; and LinkedIn allows you to do this.

LinkedIn allows you to who a person is connected to, and who you have in common, i.e., are both mutually connected to.

This is why we want to make sure we connect with every person we know and every new person we meet. We never know whom they know or whom we might know that they might like an introduction to.

Throughout our lives, we meet people and establish pockets of trust. In each different groups, community and workplace, we have a certain level of trust built up. How we conduct ourselves and what happens, creates our reputation, good or bad. This Trust is now currency we can leverage to move our careers and businesses forward.

The reputation we have built will determine whether someone is willing to introduce us to their network and to their contacts.

During our careers, we can lose business or our wealth for a multitude of reasons, but if we have a good reputation, people will always help us reclaim our lives and get back on our feet. A good reputation is the biggest asset we can probably ever have, and thus should be carefully attended to.

The art of networking, therefore, is to put our good reputation and the trust we have built, to good work. Asking for introductions is an excellent way to build our business, and for the most part, if our product and service are good, people will be willing to give them.

Before asking for an introduction, we need a good reason, something that will motivate our connection to make the introduction. This might be that they see a match between the problem they know their colleague has, or potentially has, and what you have to offer. However if the person isn't entirely convinced they have a problem that they need help with, you'll need something a lot more compelling to get the person to actually speak with you.

Having a compelling Call-to-Action that is hard to say 'no' to, will go a long way.

The Importance of a Good Diagnostic

When building a Call-To-Action, we should never assume that a person is confident to speak to us on the phone and discuss their issue.

They may be a very confident person and someone who is ready to buy a solution, however, this doesn't mean that someone won't be afraid to say 'no' to you and fear begin pushed into buying something they will later regret.

If a person isn't sure they are ready to invest in a solution, or that they would like to invest with you, then there is a good chance they won't have the conversation with you in the first place. Thus we need to give them another reason to speak to us, a reason that gives them all of the benefits and makes them feel comfortable talking to us.

When it comes to asking if someone would like to buy, you will be told 'no' if the person hasn't yet fully understood the importance of what you are offering and how it applies to them.

If someone isn't fully aware of the problem they have or the impact it is having on their life, they won't' see the value in investing their hard-earned money with you.

Thus what we need to do is give people an opportunity to explore their problem in a safe environment and understand it.

A diagnostics is the perfect way to do this and makes a great call-to-action as the value is entirely steeped in our prospects favour. They are going to learn more about themselves and receive guidance on what to do about it. In doing this with you, they will soon see you as a friend and an expert well positioned to help them.

A diagnostic should create a safe environment within which people can explore the problem without fear of being sold to. This is a premise you set up at the beginning of the diagnostic, with a script that ensures people understand what is about to happen and puts them at ease.

It creates curiosity and intrigue. It offers something that people want to find out about without there being an assumption that the person needs your services.

For example, I write people's LinkedIn profiles for them. However, most people believe their profile is fine until I show them why it is not. I don't deliberately rip it apart, I just show them there is another way to write it for business development.

When someone first comes to me, they generally don't know that they need help or that their profile is really that important. They are however curious about know how they are doing and hear what I have to say about them.

So I offer a 30-minute LinkedIn Profile Review during which I take the time to learn about a person's business, what they are trying to achieve and then provide tailored advice outlining exactly how to fix it.

The conversation provides an opportunity to explore their business and have someone reflect back on how well they are doing. We look at the business structure; the sales funnel, the packaging and how easy it is for clients to get to know them. Finding someone who will take the time out to listen to you and provide free advice is rare and often prospects tell me how refreshing it is just to be able to talk about their business openly and look at it.

In the sessions I provide my prospect all the information they need to write the profile for themselves, even detailing out how to structure their summary. I provide a huge amount of value in a short amount of time, at the end of which the prospect will either determine they can fix things up for themselves or they need my help.

By providing a clear option at the beginning, saying there is no pressure, either way, they don't have to learn how I can help them, at the very beginning of the call, I create a safe environment in which they can explore the extent of the problem – or if they already have one – and make an educated decision as to whether they should invest in a solution or continue as they are.

In my industry, there is a very high likelihood that someone I would identify as a prospect for my business would not identify them self as a prospect for me. Until they speak to me, they have no idea that this is something they need.

It is the same if you offer leadership training. Most people think they are great leaders and that their high staff turnover is because they can't get the right staff. The truth is it could well be that you're a poor leader – wouldn't you like to find out? If this is the first time you've heard this reasoning, you'll likely be raising your eyes thinking 'Really? I am the problem?' Well, wouldn't you like to find out? Come and take this diagnostic with me!

Do you see how we just manage to go from not knowing you had a leadership problem with wanting to speak to the leadership coach?

This is the impact we need to create with your profile. When people view your LinkedIn profile, do they feel excited about what you offer?

Or do people feel indifferent and even confused about you, and even wonder why someone recommended them to you?

If we leave people feeling indifferent about us, even if we know they are our prospect, a person will likely go back to doing what they were already doing - 'fire fighting'! They will go back to handling the problem thinking that is their only option, and they don't have time to speak to you who holds the magic medicine and could take away all their problems.

Instead, they will perceive that continuing to handle the consequences of their problem is a better use of time than speaking to you and getting to the source of the problem, and solve it, once and for all = because they don't believe that spending time with you will actually put the fire out. This is what we need to change.

Diagnostics makes a conversation. An exchange of value that can't be argued with, even if the conversion isn't concluded with a sales pitch at the end.

A diagnostic could be a 30-minute conversation where you diagnose the problem and offer clear advice like I provide, an online tool that provides helpful insight and guidance, or a 10-question diagnostic given over the phone.

The key is to make it compelling, so people want to say yes. If they aren't saying 'yes,' or saying 'yes' and then not showing up, there is more work to be done.

Create a Diagnostic for your Business

To find out more about creating a diagnostic that will fill your sales funnel, visit www.TheExpertEconomy.uk for more

First Impressions

When being introduced to a new prospect, you want to put your best foot forward and consider the reputation of the person introducing you. Having a professional, well-thought-out LinkedIn Profile quickly communicates the type of person you are and the quality of service the individual is likely to receive.

The important thing is to make sure that the person being refereed doesn't have to work too hard to work out why their trusted friend or colleague recommended they speak to you.

Your objective is to have the person being introduced down tools and call you immediately because they can see that by investing time and money with you, you will save them the same in the long run.

The other day, I made a referral for a friend. However it fell on deaf ears because I wasn't able to pitch their service well enough on their behalf, and I didn't have a LinkedIn profile or website to refer their prospect to help me. In this instance, a good introduction was lost.

Balancing the Product and the Person

When writing your profile, and those of your team, it is important to find the right balance between the person and the product.

A profile that talks just about the product and service with little reference to the individual do not fare well. A visitor to a profile is looking to connect with a person, someone they know or might like to get to know. They are not looking to connect with a business or be met by a marketing message.

When positioning your profile, it's wise to consider how your mother or friends would feel visiting it: Would they visit the profile and opt not to connect with you as they consider it part of your 'business persona' and not the right arena for personal relationships? Would they be able to read it and understand what it is you actually do?

Ultimately we want those who know you to recognise you – as you – and then become interested, if not energised, to tell other people about you.

When constructing a profile, we have to achieve a balance between the person, the company brand and the product being sold. If a profile is actively used as a marketing and sales tool, it must adhere to the company brand and best practice, but it must also favour the personality and voice of the individual.

A careful balance needs to be found that benefits the employee and the employer.

Recently, I worked with a large international corporation creating a profile for one of their key department heads. We worked closely with the branding team to ensure the words used toed the company line. We decided that the keywords and phrases used by the individual every day, such as 'we nail it' or 'it was like the Wild West,' couldn't be used on the profile as they didn't translate well in written form and weren't in line with the company brand.

It took a lot of debate to balance the individual's character with the company branding, but eventually, the balance was found, and all parties were happy.

Conveying your personality and your professionalism on your profile is absolutely imperative for your success on LinkedIn. Your profile contributes towards your personal brand. A poorly constructed profile with sloppy formatting can convey that you don't care about your appearance, while a well-constructed, well-thought-out profile can win you business and referrals. I often compare a poor profile to showing up to work in your pyjamas.

Social Selling: Never Just 'Sell'!

Essentially, a LinkedIn profile is a 24/7 international billboard selling your business and your solution. It should give people an insight into your philosophy, the reason why we do what we do and the impact you want to have in the world. When correctly constructed it will position you as the 'go to' expert in your industry.

In 2012, the term 'social selling' was coined to describe a new era of buying and selling via social platforms. In the early days, it was unclear how each platform would evolve and what culture each would adapt, but as time has gone on, the communities of each platform have spoken out, clearly saying what they expected from the community, which has shaped online etiquette and formed the unique culture of each platform.

In 2009, two new words became popular to describe disconnecting someone online: 'defriend' and 'unfriend.'

It quickly became clear that people did not want to be sold to on social platforms. Early-day info-products that taught on how to make money on social media quickly become out-dated.

Instead, platforms became places to meeting new people. They were not a place for selling. Facebook became a platform for friends and family, while LinkedIn became the platform to do business. Yet, neither was the place to make special offers or outright sell products.

Thus, those wishing to sell on the platform, as most of us in business attempt to do now, had to become a lot savvier.

Thus the term Social Selling emerged.

Social selling is the term used to describe selling via a social platform, and as we've outlined above, it's a lot more complex than it sounds.

The two words 'social' and 'selling' are actually polar opposites, with a substantial gap between them.

For example, if a friend rocked up to your birthday party and started giving product demonstrations to all your guests, would you be happy about it?

If you were approached by a potential business supplier while buying lunch for your family in a theme park, would you welcome the conversation or try to put the person off until Monday? And when Monday came, would you feel positive about talking to this person? Or would you feel slightly uncomfortable around them now, thinking they might be a little odd or at least, pushy?

Being social within a business context, however, is absolutely imperative. It is often the foundation for all new and lasting business relationships.

Bumping into a colleague at a theme part could actually work to your advantage, especially if you have the chance to introduce your families.

So what's the difference?

The difference is acting appropriately to the environment and respecting the maturity of the relationship.

Bumping into a colleague in a social setting is an opportunity to advance a relationship further and build vital 'know, like, trust,' but it will only work if you know how to behave appropriately in that environment.

Talking about business in a social environment might feel like an intrusion, or create tension between them and their children as they feel they have lost the attention of their parent. Instead, we need to be invited to speak about our product with a prospect in a setting that isn't necessarily about business, which is exactly what Facebook is.

I often refer to Facebook as being a theme park. There are many reasons why someone will be on the platform from social to business, and since you don't know which it is, you have to tread very carefully before opening up a business conversation.

On Facebook, we post pictures of our family, parties, our pets, and our lunch, and it is generally considered OK. However, on LinkedIn, the opposite would be considered true.

LinkedIn is the equivalent of a business-networking event, where it is generally expected that everyone behave professionally. Uploading photos of our new baby or our dinner is not considered appropriate.

The key is to know the difference between to two and act appropriately.

However even conforming to that, selling on a social platform is still not acceptable. Instead, we must cultivate relationships until it feels appropriate and natural to mention our product.

Of course, it is possible to sell directly via social media and to talk outright about your product in your status updates, the difference is how you mention them and when.

The trick is to mention the product carefully and lead people to want to find out more and thus visit your profile. When they do, they get to know more about you as a person, what you are selling and most importantly, why.

Your Social Compass

With each social platform having its own culture and etiquette, its important to adjust accordingly and respect the one you are on. What you might post on Facebook might not favour well on LinkedIn, and if it doesn't it can go seriously against you

Thus, what we need to do is understand the culture of the platform we are using, and ten use our social compass to work out what is appropriate and what is not.

If you feel uncomfortable taking action, whether that is messaging someone new or posting a photo or article, it could be nerves associated with 'putting yourself out there' but it call also be your social compass telling you it is the wrong thing to do, that this action doesn't follow normal social protocol and you should do it.

To use your social compass, simply ask yourself 'If I met this person face-to-face, would it feel normal to do this?' If the answer is no, then don't do it.

For example, if we had never met and I walked up to you at a business-networking event and instantly launched into telling you about my products and services, telling you that you absolutely had to try them out – how would you feel? Would it make you want to try my products or and want to get to know me?

It's unlikely.

No matter how compelling we feel, our offer is, if we haven't first greeted each other properly and begun a mutual conversation, there will be little chance that someone will take us up on our offer. Instead, the person will likely be thinking 'what is this person's problem?'

It is exactly the same when someone accepts our invitation to connect, and we instantly hit them with a message pitching our products without first determining if they have a need for them.

By definition, to 'sell' means to make a full presentation and then ask the buying question. To get to the state where you are invited to make a full presentation takes time and it is unlikely it will ever happen in a social setting unless someone already has identified they have a need and are proactively looking for your solution. In this case, they will let you know by asking questions of you.

Instead, for us to sell, we need to set up a selling environment, a time and place where both parties agree to come together to have a conversation about your offer. If someone is connecting with you to find out more about what you have to offer, their next step is obvious; we invite them to have a conversation with us. The difference is though, we have set up the context of the conversation, and so there are no nasty, uncomfortable surprises.

If you are connecting with someone, you will need to first build the conversation before making your request. Otherwise it will come on heavy and likely put the person off.

As you can see then, the term 'Social Selling' is a misnomer since the two words seem to contradict each other.

To succeed, therefore, we need to use our Social Compass to navigate the natural stages of relationship building, and only ask the prospect if they are interested in learning about our product when it feels natural, or we have identified and helped them realise, there is a need.

The word that binds 'Social Selling' together is the word 'relationship.' Social selling is possible when you first know how to build the relationship.

Once we have someone's interest and permission to move the conversation forward, we can ask them to attend a webinar, download a report or arrange a diagnostic call with us.

By sharing great content that adds value, we help our marketplace identify their problem and diagnose it; we then create a need within them to find out more. If we can match that with a compelling call-to-action that makes it easy for someone to find out more, we're winning. However, we should never outright tell someone they have a problem.

Another new term that has become popular is 'human to human.' It replaces the term 'business to business' and 'business to consumer,' placing relationship and connection at the heart of the transaction. It goes hand in hand with the term 'people buy people.'

One of the most powerful ways to move a relationship forward on a social media platform is to get off it.

Yep, you read that right. As soon as you have someone's interest, transfer your conversations to either the telephone or a face-to-face meeting. Conversations that are drawn out on social media conversation threads tend to go cold quickly, and not result in your outcome.

Thus we need to move the conversation forward and invite them to take action outside of the platform. Depending on our business, this might be to enter our automated sales funnel by downloading a book or report, or it might be to book a physical appointment with us on the phone or in-person depending on which feels most appropriate.

2. Using LinkedIn

One of the biggest obstacles I see for people considering using LinkedIn is the perception of how much time it takes and the fear it won't produce results. They fear that if they take their eyes off the normal, old ways of doing things, and the new thing doesn't work, they'll end up with nothing.

Sometimes it seems easy to just stick to what we know than to risk learning something new

Is LinkedIn a Productivity Tool or a Time Vampire?

When using LinkedIn, the starting point is always to consider the results you want to create.

If you are a high-volume business needing a lot of new clients each month, you'll need to spend much more time on the platform than someone who needs fewer clients to reach capacity within their business.

With so many things you could be doing on the platform, the key is to have a clear outcome and know exactly what you are there to achieve. We've already said that we aren't going to achieve sales on LinkedIn, but that we can be social and we can invite people to speak to us about what we offer.

This is what we need to focus on when interacting on LinkedIn. We need to focus on developing relationships and maturing them to the point where the person is happy to have a sales conversation, our diagnostic.

When we hold this firmly in our minds, we'll naturally take the actions that lead us to that outcome and not get distracted.

When getting started with LinkedIn it can feel hard to know where to start. Just like driving a car, but what I have found is most people are having more success on the platform than they are giving themselves credit for. New assignments and commissions are coming about through relationship with people they are connected with, but because they follow the natural stages of relationships building, they don't necessary attribute the result to LinkedIn.

The steps they took, the conversations they had, what they said and did, were all natural parts of how they build relationships.

Success with LinkedIn isn't about having success in isolation of any other part of how we normally win business.

Rather, LinkedIn compliments and speeds up or results, and increase our potential to succeed. LinkedIn gives us the opportunity to accelerate our results, cross barriers and enter conversations we wouldn't have otherwise been able to.

Taking the time to master the platform is imperative, as well as cultivating the right strategy for using it. Just like a car you need to know how to drive it if you're going to get the advantages. And just like driving you to need to have a destination and a plan for getting there. The investment of your times is always worth it. Just like learning to drive has saved us all plenty of time and allowed us to travel further and achieve more than our predecessors, so too can LinkedIn help us in our business.

Used well LinkedIn is the best productivity tool you'll ever find. Used poorly, without a strategy and a clear goal, it'll be the big time waster as it sucks you into its vortex of unending content.

If you feel that LinkedIn is just another thing on your never-ending list of things to do or you feel you don't have enough time, then I suggest as a minimum you write a great profile. Often I get very busy in my business and take my eyes off cultivating new relationships, but I always find new leads arrive for the simple reason that my profile is always working for me.

It only takes a few minutes a day to respond to invitations and post a quick update; actions that pay dividends when your profile pitches what you do and why someone should work with you.

A little while back I had coffee with a lady who was starting a new business. She was rather pleased with herself because she had purchased a list of all the businesses in her area that she could approach with her services. She planned to get in contact with each and introduce herself. However, the list didn't have telephone numbers or the names of the people she needed to approach. Plus it was six months old.

I asked her if she'd like an up-to-date list that included the names of the people she needed to speak to, and even analysis on whom in her network knew the person so she could ask for an introduction. She got very excited. So I told to use LinkedIn!

How to Create More Revenue in Less Time

A good business is one that offers an exceptional product or service to clients who are willing to pay for it.

If you want to charge a high price, then you need to identify the people with the ability to pay the price you are asking, and package your services to solve a big problem worthy of the amount you are asking.

Or if you want to offer a middle of the range price, you apply the same strategy by identifying exactly who needs your solution and why they need to invest in it.

When we do this, we can pitch our services at the right level.

To be successful, surely all we need to do is find the right target market and pitch our services to them? If we pitch enough, we can guarantee that a certain portion all people will buy from us (our sales conversion rate).

If we want to generate more revenue in less times, we simply need to make sure we go on appointments with the ideal clients who are able to pay for our services and that we are charging the right amount of money.

Let's examine different scenarios.

Say you're attending 10 sales appointments per week with less-than-ideal prospects. You're able to convert 30% into a sale for an average value of £500. You, therefore, have a weekly income of £1500.

To increase your weekly sales income, you have four options:

1. Attend more appointments.

If you achieve five more appointments per week (a total of 15) and continue to convert at 30%, you will now achieve 4.5 sales and earn £2500 per week.

2. Attend appointments with ideal clients.

You identify exactly who your ideal client is and how they tend to decide to purchase a product like yours. You create the right resources for them, and they come to your business pre-sold. You continue to have 10 appointments per week, but now you have a conversion rate of 70%. Based on your original price, you are now earing £3500.

You could also improve your chances of an increased conversion by investing in your sales skills.

3. Attend more appointments with ideal clients.

Now it is important to target the right audience, as this will lead to a better sales conversion, and the more appointments of this callibre lead, the more revenue you will make. Instead of attending 10 appointments you now attend 15 and convert 70% at

£500 each, winning 10 sales per week and earning £5000.

4. You Increase Your Price

   You target better clients, increase your sales conversion and increase your price to £2500 by of creating a package that solves a bigger problem for your clients in one hit. You now attend 15 sales appointments, win 10 sales per week at £2500 earning you £25000 per week.

The following graph assumes an increase in sales conversion from 30% to 70% from our original weekly revenue of £1500.

	Same Appointments	Increased Appointments
Increased Value	£17,500	£25,000
Same Value	£3500	£5000

With these simple changes, we can dramatically change our earnings. With free platforms like LinkedIn, a clear pitch and helping our target market achieve 57% of their buying decision independent of our time, we can dramatically increase our conversion rate and thus our revenue.

When we add to improve our packages and thus the price that we can charge, the number goes through the roof.

By carefully positioning our business and leveraging the trust in our network, we can quickly find ourselves having more appointments with our target clients. And since LinkedIn is free, we can achieve this with little to no investment in the initial stages!

By establishing a good LinkedIn profile, you can quickly put yourself back in the driving seat of your business, no longer reliant on word of mouth.

Getting Results on LinkedIn

There are plenty of strategies and tactics you can use on LinkedIn, but the key is to identify the right ones for you, the ones that will create the outcomes you want to achieve. As your business progresses, your outcomes will likely change.

It is important to be flexible and know the business you're in and the etiquette associated with it. Social selling is about relationships, so to succeed, you need to care about your prospects and their success genuinely.

The key to success is to know your outcome, apply the right strategies at the right time and leverage the trust in your network.

The Evolution of Your Profile

The great thing about your LinkedIn profile is that it is easy to change, and thus, as your business evolves, making updates is quick and simple. If you're just starting out in business, LinkedIn completely eradicates the initial need for a website and branding, which are big investments for any business but even more so to one that doesn't know yet who its ideal clients are or what appeals to them.

In my first book, *Grassroots to Green Shoots*, I talk about how you can't stand over a plant and shout 'grow!' and expect it to do so, or how if you plan a new seed in the ground, you can't expect fruit instantly. It takes time.

For those getting started, LinkedIn gives you the space to grow into your business and the time to discover what it is going to be. It gives you the opportunity to position yourself as an expert while remaining authentic as a new startup. By doing so, we can command authority and attention, and leverage the trust in our network, opening more doors than if we pretend to have all our ducks lined up.

That is our **new starter strategy**.

If you're an affiliate marketer, you can easily add a new venture to your profile—though you'll want to be careful about your branding and consider how you position it among your other activities to avoid detracting from your core business. There are many ways you can add it to your profile, in line with your branding and in a way that pays dividends.

That is our **affiliate marketing strategy**.

If you have a new take on how something should be done—whether it be finances, childcare, or business—and insights you're burning to share with other people, LinkedIn is the perfect place to connect with others who are on the same path as you or are interested in a new way of doing things. You can quickly establish yourself as a thought leader and the go-to person in your industry by using your LinkedIn profile.

That is our **thought leadership strategy**.

If you're already established in business with plenty of new opportunities coming to you, you can retain your status, keep demand at a high level, and have your clients come to you eager to work with you and follow your directions by ensuring your profile is continually in line with your personal brand and adds to, rather than detracts from, your other marketing materials.

This is our **established expert strategy**.

If you're an organisation looking to attract top talent and leverage the trust of your employees, creating great profiles that reflect the personality and values of each individual and those of the company as a whole will pay dividends with greater client engagement, rapport, and enthusiasm.

This is our **business team strategy**.

In this book, I give you insider information on how to create an engaging profile that achieves the outcomes you want to achieve and creates the business you deserve.

As we've seen, there are three types of strategies on LinkedIn: passive, active, and proactive. The passive strategy is to maintain a LinkedIn profile. We've also seen the financial benefits of making sure your profile reflects exactly what you do and the value you provide.

Since you are always developing, your profile will be developing along with you. Therefore, this book is split into three key sections that will allow you to build your profile up gradually. We start with your strategy, and the basics you'll want to make sure are in place. Then we build up to more advanced activities that take a little more time and attention and promote business clarity.

GET IN TOUCH

If you are a business owner, thought leader, or start-up entrepreneur and are unsure how to build your profile and would benefit from a chat, why not get in touch with one of our consultants?

Our appointments are 100% strategy-based, designed to help you get as much direction as possible.

And if you should need it, we're on hand to write your profile for you! Just give us a call and let's see if we can help you!

DOWNLOAD OUR FREE LINKEDIN PROFILE TEMPLATE BUILDER

As a special gift, we'd like to offer you our LinkedIn Profile Template Builder, which maps out each section of a profile so you can organise and draft your content before publishing it online.

To download, go to
www.TheProfile.Company.

Exercise: Effortlessly Increase Your Sales Revenue

With the clients you currently work with, what is your average sale value (the average amount someone spends with you)?

$a =$

How many sales appointments do you currently attend per week?

$b =$

Of those appointments, how many people purchase from you?

$p =$

If you were working with your ideal client, what would your average sales value be (the amount you would like to charge on average for each client)?

$i =$

How many appointments per week could you be attending?

$c =$

Now let's work this out. Let's calculate:

Your average current weekly income:

$a \times p =$

What would happen if you increased appointments?

$a \times c =$

What would happen if you met only your ideal clients?

$i \times p =$

What if you increased appointments and met only your ideal clients?

$i \times c =$

	Same Appointments	Increased Appointments
Increased Value	$i \times p$	$i \times c$
Same Value	$a \times p$	$a \times c$

Fill in your own numbers:

	Same Appointments	Increased Appointments
Increased Value		
Same Value		

3. Strategy

Ideally, once complete, your profile should be a case of set-and-forget. You will need to review it every couple of months to ensure it's evolving with your business and still reflecting your key message, but generally it is static and rarely requires daily updates.

When putting your profile together, you need to ask yourself two questions:

- What does my target audience need to know about me to be interested in what I have to offer?

- What action do I want people to take as a result of coming to my profile?

Target Audience

One of the most common mistakes people make in their LinkedIn profiles is to write them for themselves. Let's get one thing straight right now: if you're going to be successful on LinkedIn, you need to get to the point quickly and write for your audience. Your profile isn't about your interests or hobbies. While it is *your* profile, you need to remember it is a marketing tool. And, as with any marketing activity, you need to be continually thinking about your target audience and what will catch their interest.

The standard question most people ask themselves tends to be: 'What do I want people to know about me?' However, the question we want to be asking is actually the reverse:

What do people need to know about me to be interested in my services?

With 550+ million LinkedIn profiles in existence and just as many status updates per day, LinkedIn is a busy place. If someone lands on your profile the question the only question they are asking is 'is this relevant to me?' It's just like walking down a busy street. We simply don't have time to speak to every person and inquire about him or her. It is just the same on LinkedIn. We will only read profiles that grab our attention and appear relevant to us.

A profile that is written like a CV, will only be read by someone in recruitment. This is true even if a person met you at a networking event and wants to follow up with you. They will glance at it and think 'this isn't relevant to me' and move on. They will still connect with you, they will still follow up with you, but they will consider it an ineffective resource not to be used. Thus we lose a vital opportunity to continue our conversation with our prospect, build our authority on the subject and get referred.

An effective profile will capture the attention of each of these different mindsets and excites the prospect as to what's possible.

Your profile is your business pitch, and just like when you stand in front of investors or meet someone for the first time, you need to come straight to the point about the problem you solve, the value you bring, and how you deliver.

Your profile needs to quickly establish you as an expert in your field, demonstrating that you understand the unique challenges involved. You need to exhibit your credentials, your proven history in delivering a return on investment, and the value that you add.

Remember that people are busy. They have a problem, and they are busy managing it. When challenged with a problem, they are often busy, stressed, and firefighting. The last thing they want is an unwelcome interruption. Your goal is to be a welcome interruption and dangle a sparkling carrot in front of them that draws their attention and makes them want to take action.

How People Buy

Instead, we need to write for our prospect and appeal to them. To do this, we need to consider where they are in their buying journey. In the following diagram I outline the process prospects go through when making a buying decision. A profile needs to complete each stage of the journey to be effective.

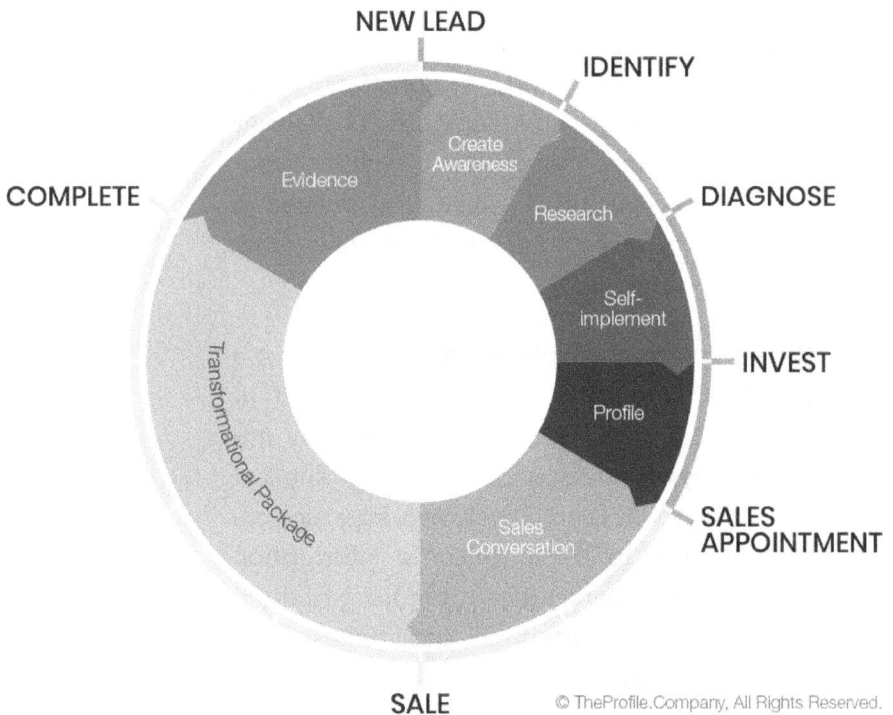

NEW LEAD

IDENTIFY

COMPLETE

DIAGNOSE

Create Awareness

Evidence

Research

Self-implement

INVEST

Transformational Package

Profile

SALES APPOINTMENT

Sales Conversation

SALE

© TheProfile.Company, All Rights Reserved.

NEW LEAD: Social Media has made it possible to appeal to a prospect who don't yet know they have a problem that needs solving. Previously our marketing would only reach prospects that had to identify they had a problem and were in the process of researching solutions using keywords. Now, however, we can pitch our message to a wide variety of people who aren't actively looking for solutions and awaken them to the fact that actually what they are experiencing is really a symptom of a problem that could easily be solved.

IDENTIFY: Once the person has identified they may have a problem they will begin researching it in order to define what the problem is and fully diagnose it.

DIAGNOSE: Once the person is sure they have the problem and are clear on what it is and the impact it is having on them, they will begin to research solution and implement them independently. It is only when they realise that they can't do this entirely alone, that the problem is bigger than them and requires more than the free advice available online, that they will consider investing in a solution.

INVEST: Once a person has decided to invest in a solution, it will come down to who they trust to help them. This could be someone they know well or someone they have built trust with online digesting their content. If you have covered each part of the buying journey successfully, that person will be you.

SALES APPOINTMENT: Now they have decided that they want to invest in a solution and that you could be the right person, they will need to speak to you. In a time sensitive business this conversation needs to have direction and a clear structure. It needs to walk the prospect back over the buying journey, so they are reassured they have made the right conclusions, and for you, that this is someone who really needs your help.

How People Buy

If you would like to learn more about positioning yourself as a 'go to' expert and creating resources that naturally lead people to want to work with you, and how to structure the sales conversation, visit www.TheExpertEconomy.com

Action You Want People to Take

An effective profile is one that leads your prospect to take the action you set out. Whether that will be joining your mailing list or asking you for an appointment to discuss their problem.

To do this, we need to write the profile to match how people buy.

Ultimately we want all prospects to join our mailing list and benefit from our content, but it is only our most ideal clients that we want reaching out for an appointment.

To do this, we need to create a profile that easily directs people into our sales pipeline.

Today there are plenty of ways a person can get in contact with you but in our time sensitive businesses we want to make sure that only those that know they are ready to buy get in touch with us.

We achieve this by supplying all the information they would need on our LinkedIn profile. If you find people are calling you with small questions, review your profile and your website to see if you are actually answering the questions within the content. If not update your content so people can find answers without calling.

People today expect to find these answers online, and if they don't, there is a high likelihood they will Google the answer and land on your competitor's site and buy from them. If they do call, you'll also find that they are only interested in receiving an answer to their question and not open to a lengthy chat.

What we want is people getting in touch who are ready to explore working with you and have a good sense that they like you and can see themselves working with you.

How People Read Profiles

When someone lands on your profile, they are in the scan-reading mode, and until they see something that catches their interest they aren't going to stop and read. Instead, they will scan it over to decipher what this profile is about and if it is relevant to them.

They will make quick assumptions based on the use of keywords, length and balance of paragraph, capital letters, and amount written on the profile, which indicates how much care you have taken putting it together.

The natural flow a person takes through a profile is as follows:

Discovers profile

Headline

Summary (2 lines)

Experience (first 3)

Rich Content Media

Testimonials

Call to
Action

As with any marketing activity, you need each item to be captivating enough to intrigue the person to move to the next item. This is why in this book, we're looking at every one of these areas.

Notice too that the above diagram doesn't exactly follow the order of items on LinkedIn. Although rich content media (slideshows, videos, PowerPoint presentations, book samples, etc.) can appear under most sections of the profile, generally people won't engage with them until they feel confident that they are worth clicking on. First, they do a quick scan of the profile, gathering as much information as possible before investing time in taking a look at them.

EXAMPLE: Get Your Prospects Curious to Know More

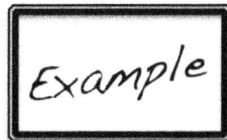

Example

A few months back, a colleague of mine received an In-Mail from someone he didn't know. Like most of us, sales message from people we don't know, tend to get ignored. However, in this email, the sender provided him with just the right amount of information to make him curious enough to click on the link provided.

Clicking on the link, Mike was led to watch a short video presentation that, again, made him curious. This was followed by another video, a short message, and a request to discuss the opportunity further.

Within just five minutes, Mike found himself booking an appointment to speak to the person who five minutes ago was a complete stranger intruding upon his busy schedule.

The key, therefore, is to peak someone's curiosity and make it easy to opt into each item of content and then feel grateful for the opportunity to speak to you.

On social media, the last thing you want to do is ask too much of your new contact before you have established a need.

This really is social selling at its best, and it can be replicated by anyone using their LinkedIn profile.

Each part of your profile needs to intrigue, offering the visitor something more that will lead them to want to know more. When done correctly and with personality, you'll be building rapport with your visitor and starting a relationship.

Easy First Yes

The key to keeping your prospect engaged is to never ask too much of them. Each step needs to be logical, building upon the last piece of information supplied and establishing trust.

Each request to take the next step needs to feel easy and non-imposing. It needs to establish credibility and authority.

The other week I received a very friendly email from someone saying they were coming to London and would I like to travel up from the south coast to meet her. She would be more than happy to shout me a coffee and a muffin. Only I had no idea whom she was or what the conversation would be about.

I replied and asked if we knew each other. She said we did not, but she ran a software company in Poland and would I come and meet her.

My answer was no. I wasn't being mean, but to travel several hours to the city to have a conversation about something I didn't even know was relevant to me was a really big ask.

While she had personalised her request to acknowledge my location, she set no context for what we might talk about or what problem she might solve or opportunity she might create in our meeting.

A request needs to be simple and easy to say yes to. It needs to appeal to your busy prospect and provide a compelling reason to meet. Via message, this might need to be done in several stages as with the example above.

When building your LinkedIn profile, you need to replicate the conversation you would have with a prospect if you met at a networking event or if you were going back and forth with several messages to peak their interest.

You need to take a prospect from not knowing they have a problem to need your solution, to knowing they have a problem and jumping through hoops to speak to you.

We do this by handling objections upfront and before the prospect asks. Questions they will be asking include:

- Have I got time for this, or is my time better spent elsewhere?

- Do I feel comfortable scheduling a phone consultation or a face-to-face meeting?

- What value will this bring me?

- Are you a credible authority on this topic?

- Is speaking to you more important than the zillion other things I have to do?

Get this right, and your first contact with someone will be a promising conversation and an invitation to pitch your services.

If your Call-to-Action is to spend time with you, then you need to outline the value the person will receive during the call and what to expect. They will also need to feel comfortable divulging sensitive information about their company or their life to you. This trust needs to be developed in your profile.

At this point they aren't ready to buy from you, they are just ready to explore the issues they have and how you might work together.

The appointment should be about listening to your prospect and gathering information so you can make a relevant and personalized presentation as to why your proposition is right for them.

I provide more insight into how to achieve this within my book The Expert Economy. If you would like to learn how to do it like a pro, then I invite you to join my LinkedIn Business Strategy Course.

Advancing the Sales Conversation

Your time is precious, so you don't want to be spending it on educating people on basic industry information if a video presentation can do it for you. If the information you have to share is of a basic nature, the conversation is likely to end with the person feeling overwhelmed by their new learning and in need of some time to digest all that you've said and get a handle on it.

In these cases, the sale is unlikely to happen that day.

If the information you are providing is content you find you are continually repeating, then this is the type of thing you can turn into a quick video or ebook.

By having it in place, you can make reading/watching it a prerequisite for a meeting or simply direct people to it in the interim between booking and having the meeting. You can also use it as a helpful follow-up resource.

It'll never be an exact science but having it will help you greatly in your sales process and lead to more advanced sales conversations and better-educated clients. You'll close deals faster and free up more time.

Tip...

TIP: Use Rich Media to Advance the Sales Conversation

Creating a video or ebook will help you advance the conversation with prospects leading them to be better educated about your solution by the time you speak.

You might email: 'Hi, [name]. I'd love to have a chat with you. Let's get a date in the diary, and in the meantime, why don't you watch this video? It will answer some of your questions and help us get more from our conversation.'

Advancing the Buying Decision Further

When companies make decisions, they often involve several people. If someone is commissioned with the job of finding a solution, they are likely to research various solutions and present back. Before meeting with a prospect or being invited to a meeting with the company, wouldn't it be great to know that the senior decision makers have been given your full business information?

By supplying useful content on your LinkedIn profile and web page, you can attend the meetings knowing that the senior decision makers have received the best information about your business that reflects well on your brand.

Therefore, when creating the content for your website, you need to consider what the researcher needs to know to start their decision-making process and how they will present your information to their senior manager. The more you help the researcher to answer your decision makers questions and making them look like an internal hero, the more chance you will have at succeeding.

EXAMPLE: Provide for the Messenger

Once, I received a request for a quote on in-house training. The request was rather like asking, 'How long is a piece of string?' I couldn't answer the question intelligently as I needed to know more, so I asked to have a conversation with the person. My request was denied with a counter-request just to send the information.

A little time went by, and I noticed that the lady hadn't replied to my request to just talk it through. I decided to follow up and do some investigation, and I soon learned she was an intern researching on her company's behalf. Picking up the phone to contact her, I discovered she had since left the company, giving her research findings to her manager, whom I was now speaking to. The manager had the research findings in front of her and said our information was not in the folder.

It quickly became very apparent to me how we were unwittingly missing out on valuable business. It wasn't the first time I'd had interactions with an intern conducting research.

To serve our in-house clients, we really have to speak to them in depth about their needs, but this is not a conversation an intern can have. They simply don't have the knowledge base. In this instance, what is required is valuable information that can be submitted to the manager for further consideration, and the better we can supply this information, the more we'll stand out.

By supplying this information and making it readily available, we give ourselves the best chance of being considered by those actively searching. Although this information is basic and not comprehensive enough to get a decision made, it needs to exist to get the discussion started.

At all times, your profile and supporting resources should consider the needs of different audiences. For example, an individual may wish to undertake some important training, but they need to convince the budget holder to allow them to invest in it. This won't be just about the money or you as a training provider but, in many cases, about the need for training in the first place. Your materials, therefore, need to demonstrate the return of investment for the training and exactly why it is necessary. By making this information readily available in an easy format, you're making it easier for the individual to get approval for their purchase or for the decision maker to agree to the need and consult with you as a provider.

Designing Your Profile

When designing your profile, you'll want to be asking yourself these questions:

Where are my ideal prospects?

What action do I want them to take as a result of coming to my profile?

What information do they need to know to make a buying decision?

What are the common questions I hear a lot from my prospects that I can answer online?

What are the concepts I want my prospects to know about before speaking to me that will aid them in the buying decision?

Who are the different people involved in making this decision, and what information do they need?

4. How to Use This Book

This book is split up into three sections Basic, Intermediate and Advanced. To build out your profile, it is worth starting with the Basics and working your way forward, no matter how far advanced you already are setting up your profile. This is because each piece weaves into the next and cannot be taken in isolation.

Instead, it is worth reading the theory and strategy for each element before moving forward.

From time to time LinkedIn does change, but the general set-up does not. If you are ever confused about a section and how it appears on your screen, please reach out by visiting www.TheProfile.Company where you'll likely find a blog post updating you or we can submit your question for us to answer.

We have included pictures throughout the sections as per LinkedIn's structure updates in 2017.

A WARNING

WARNING: Switch Off Profile Updates

When you make changes to your profile, your network will be notified. To avoid irritating your network or drawing attention to things you don't wish too, make sure you switch off these notifications.

To change your notification setting click on the thumbnail of your profile in the top right of your profile. In the dropdown box that appears, click on 'Privacy and Settings.'

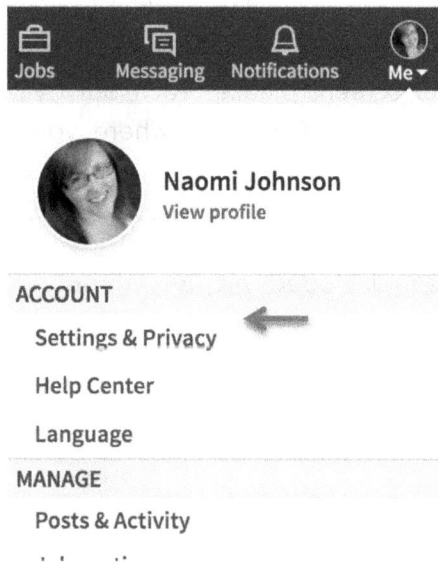

Next, navigate to the third option 'Privacy.'

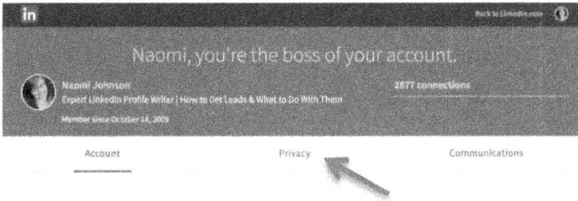

In the options below, you will see 'Sharing Profile Edits' with a slider button for Yes or No.

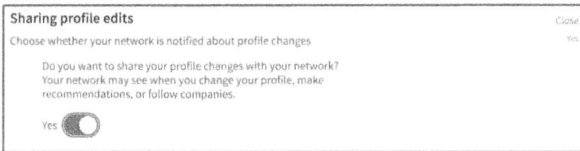

If you do not want edits to appear in your connection's notification click 'No'. Once complete click on 'Back to LinkedIn.com' at the top of the profile.

However, you do have the option with various sections to switch them back on for individual updates.

With 'Experience' you will see the option at the bottom of the editing box.

However, you will not be able to do this for Summary and no matter which option is set within settings; it will still say you can not send a notification of changes.

When you make big important changes to your profile, it is worth setting your

89

notifications to 'on' so people come and have a look. However, I would also wait until the entire profile is set up to make the impact you intend.

5. Profile Basics

Presentation is everything, and you've got less than 10 seconds to make a good impression. Beyond capturing your profile visitors' attention to deliver your message, your first goal is to convey a professional, well-constructed profile. Some of the points below may seem basic, but you'll be surprised how easy they are to commit, and the last thing you want is a warm prospect to go cold over a simple typo (yes, this happens). We've all turned our noses up at an out-of-date website or a profile full of errors and made negative assumptions about the person behind it. The following points, no matter how fundamental, are the foundations of a good profile.

Capital Letters

On your LinkedIn profile, it's imperative to have capital letters everywhere your high-school teacher taught you to put them. Some believe not having them is a style choice. However, on LinkedIn, you don't have the benefit of different fonts, colours, and sizes to present text the way you intend. Instead, to the average bystander, it simply looks like you either don't know proper English or just don't care enough about your profile—both of which are things you don't want your prospects to conclude about you.

Therefore, it is important to keep to what's expected. The important thing to remember is that it's not about you. Your profile is for your target audience, whether they be future customers, investors or colleagues. LinkedIn is a professional environment, and you need to play by the rules in the game of perception.

Typos

So easily done yet so distracting. Make sure you ask a friend, colleague, or family member to look over your work and pay particular attention to headlines. It's not unheard of for people to write their name incorrectly or even write 'manger' instead of 'manager.' If something is supposed to be written a certain way, consider putting it in brackets or quotes to highlight this.

Spacing

Paragraph spacing makes up a lot of the visual content of your profile and is where most of the first assumptions about you are made. The key is to be consistent and think of the reader.

When filling out your Experience section try to keep to equal lengths to create a balanced feel. Generally, four to five lines of text make a 'readable' paragraph. Longer paragraphs turn off the reader as they tend to require more effort to follow, especially on screen.

For your summary, shorter paragraphs that draw people in and replicate a conversation work. Don't be afraid to have a paragraph of just one word or sentence, i.e. 'and we're on a mission to change this'. It is all about conversation and pace. Splitting the text down will ensure people can read it easily and be drawn to your key messages.

Consistency is really important as it shows that you've applied great thought and care to your profile. Try to keep bullet points tidy and if using subheadings create a style that makes things stand out, like capital letters.

Often, we can't see bad formatting or untidiness ourselves, so it's always best to ask someone else to give it a fresh look-over from a visual perspective.

Quality Photo

LinkedIn is a professional website where people expect to do business with you. Therefore, a professional photo is required. Avoid casual photos taken at social events, photos where you've cut your friends out, or those where the background has too much texture, like at the kitchen table or in the hallway. A picture is worth a thousand words, and you want to avoid saying anything more than your professional message. Whether consciously or unconsciously, the human eye is taking it all in and making judgments and assumptions.

Changes to LinkedIn in 2017 saw the profile picture reduce in size, making it harder to see a person if there is too much background. Therefore the best headshots are now simply that. The head. Try to avoid too much background and ensure your face is the only thing in the frame.

Trimming photos within LinkedIn has become increasingly difficult, so to avoid time I suggest cropping the photo in other software first. When hiring a photographer make sure they understand how important this shot is and the need to crop around your face.

Even though we see a lot less of the photo now here are some things to consider:

Message

Interestingly, how the photo is taken also affects whether someone will want to contact you. A warm, friendly, inviting smile can make a person feel welcome to make contact, whereas a stern photo may make a person think twice. If you're the CEO you may not want everyone connecting with, and then only those who operate at a certain level, so a more professional stern photo might be what you need.

If you're in the coaching business, your first contact with someone is likely to require them to reveal personal information to you, so a smiling close-up photo can help the person feel more familiar and at ease with you.

Credibility

As I pointed out before, a photo speaks a thousand words—even about your ability to do a job. If you saw a photo that was clearly taken in the 80s or had an 80s style, would you trust the person with building your new, cutting-edge website or mobile phone app? Not likely. A photo instantly communicates the 'old days' will lead a person to question if you're as up to date as you need to be.

On one occasion, I spoke to a gentleman who looked very young in his profile and hadn't filled out much of his profile. When I dialled his number to call him for his appointment, I figured he was the intern, and I wasn't too enthusiastic about speaking to him. During the call, though, I was extremely aware that I was asking questions suited to a junior employee rather than a senior director.

I soon discovered that, in fact, he was quite senior in the company and a lot older than I believed him to be.

While giving my client tips on his profile, I decided to be completely straight with him. I asked what he thought of the tone of my conversation and the level of my questions, and then pointed out I was treating him like a low-level intern who didn't know anything because that's whom I believed I was phoning. I also pointed out that this impression was created entirely by his profile. Even after learning about his seniority, I still found it hard to shift my perception of him.

When our profiles are completed incorrectly and have a misleading photo, we make our jobs harder.

Recognition

Keeping your photo up-to-date also helps you with networking. A photo that is a true reflection of what you look like (on a good day, of course) helps people to recognise you, either in person when meeting you, or in matching your profile to the person, they met at a networking event or conference. It's important to make it easy for people to find you.

Not having a photo puts you at a disadvantage. Earlier this year I spend two days at a conference sat next to the same person, but four weeks later when they sent me a friend request, I had no idea who they were. Firstly their profile didn't reflect what they were promoting, and secondly, they didn't have a photo for me to recognise them by. A picture goes a long way to building your network and giving people the confidence they are connecting with the right person.

Connection

Photos also determine how connected someone feels to you. An important part of relationship building.

I have found a stark difference between how I feel about someone with a clear photo compared to someone with a distant photo or no photo at all.

Without a photo I find I have to work harder to build rapport with someone and build the relationship, often I feel slightly frustrated in the conversation.

During one call I was having a particularly difficult time relating to a person, and to help me I began clicking through their website to help add to what they were telling me. When I landed on their website biography with a huge smiling picture of the person, I instantly felt the relationship transform. The person was no longer distant to me but close.

Photos need to be close up headshots that clearly show your facial features. With LinkedIn's changes, be particular sure to have the frame tight to your face.

Over the next week, as you engage with people on LinkedIn, take time to recognise how you feel about a person because of their LinkedIn photo. Start to be aware of your reactions, as subtle as they may be, and how you feel about different people. Correlate this with how you met, the information available and also how tangible they feel from their photo. The differences are subtle but powerful.

Use this as the basis for how you construct your profile and how you convey yourself in your photo.

Technical

For the perfect upload, your photos need to have high resolution, up to 4 MB. On the profile, there is an option for visitors to click to see a larger version of your photo. So makes sure it doesn't lose quality by uploading a quality photo.

It is also possible to select who can see your photo, and restrict it to just first- or second-degree contacts. Many people feel safer with this option, and of course, it's entirely up to you and what you feel is appropriate for your objective. As we've mentioned, having a photo available for all to see has its own advantages.

Name

2

Firstly, make sure it's yours. OK, obvious point. Strangely, your name is another area where you want to make sure you've spelled it correctly. It's interesting to see the number of people who inadvertently have a typo in this section.

Changed your name recently?

If you recently got married and changed your name, you'll want to help your network by letting them know. You can do this by formatting your name as follows:

Sally (Jones) Smith

This is important as the real value from LinkedIn comes from the depth of your relationships. You may not have spoken to someone for 10 years, and you may not have invited them to your wedding, yet the bond can still be strong enough for someone to want to connect with you again and could go on to be a valuable business connection. Therefore, you want to make it easy for them.

Unusual spelling or nickname

If you have a nickname or it's common to shorten your name, like Michael to Mike or James to Jim, you want to make sure people can still find you. Therefore, you'll want to include both spellings:

Michael (Mike) Clark

If your name has an unusual spelling or it's common for people to misspell your name, you want to make sure you are still found. One of my colleagues has listed all possible variations of his name from the common to the bizarre and added them to discreetly to an entry in Experience that isn't so prominent. This allows for the search engines to still find him even if the name is spelled incorrectly.

3

Company Logos

Logos on your profile are extremely important as, along with adding colour and interest to your profile, they allow people to quickly recognise the brands you have worked for and, if you work for yourself, re-enforcing your brand presence and helps get it known.

If you haven't yet begun using your Company Page think about how you would like to use it first before you start writing it. It is OK to create a page and not add content to it immediately, but starting to post and then stopping could reflect badly on your brand. Think about how you might like to use it first and how regular you will be at posting. If you are posting regularly on Facebook, you'll have no trouble adding content to LinkedIn as you can use the same content as a minimum.

Avoid adding the company logo as a graphic using the Rich Content Media section. If it asks you to upload the logo while editing your personal profile or suggests adding a link, you are probably in the wrong place. Uploading it this way will attach it as an item of media under the entry for that section, but it will have no hyperlink properties and add nothing to the profile, but the feeling of untidiness.

For previous employers, make sure to link with the official company page as this also helps LinkedIn to identify people you might want connected with, helping you to build your network quickly.

If you have employee's past and present, asking them to connect to the official company page will help to boost your exposure.

You'll want first to be sure that your company profile is of a certain standard before requesting people to update their experience as when they do so, the change will show up in their activity feed again, promoting your company and its message far and wide.

There are plenty of great Active and Proactive strategies you can use once your company page is a certain standard. As a basic make sure the page has up-to-date information, a clear description of the company that pitches what you do with a strong call to action.

How?

HOW: Adding Your Company Logo to Your Profile

To complete this section, a LinkedIn company profile must already exist for the company.

1. Open the entry in the Experience section that you want to change by clicking the blue-pencil.

2. Delete the name already written in the company name box.

3. Begin typing the company name until the correct company appears in the drop-down list.

4. Select the company from the list and save.

Edit experience   ✕

Title

Expert LinkedIn Profile Writer

Company

P The Profile Company

    P   The Profile Company
        Marketing and Advertising

       The Profile Page Testing Company
        Biotechnology

      PROFILE - THE BUSINESS SOLUTIONS COMPANY LIMITED
        Computer Software

      The Audience Profile Company B.V.

☑ I currently work here

☐ Update my industry

☐ Update my headline

If for any reason your company doesn't appear in the dropdown box, check that you have actually set the page up correctly or that you are typing it exactly as it appears on the actual page.

Unfortunately, you can no longer edit the name that appears, so if you worked for a company 20 years ago that has now been taken over by a new company and an old company page was never made, you will have to attach to the new one. You can correct any misleading implication, when you worked there and the change in the description.

Contact Information

4

Making it easy for your prospects to contact you is important. After all, it's the very reason you're here designing your profile. By giving prospects access to your contact information, you're giving them the chance to enquire and advance the conversation at their pace. By providing multiple ways of doing so, you're allowing them to do it in a way that's comfortable and natural to them.

Within the contact information, there are several fields to fill in, though you don't have to fill them all in. Leaving them blank isn't a problem, as LinkedIn just won't publish that option.

However, you should choose the fields to complete by again considering your audience and what is appropriate within your business context.

If you are not in a customer-facing role, then you'll want to consider where you want to direct service-based enquiries or new business leads within the company.

As the manager of a company or team, you'll need to think this through as you won't want new sales leads having initial contact with a shy administrator who isn't trained to handle enquires professionally.

You'll also want to consider the nature of your business, the level of existing competition, and the mindset your prospect is in when looking for a solution.

For some products and services, such as plumbing, carpet cleaning, fire training, sending a personalised invitation to connect and then waiting five days for a reply is an ineffective solution. When people want immediate answers, they want to be able to call. Therefore you need to make your phone number obvious on the profile by writing it clearly in the Summary, Experience entry for the role and the Contact Information section.

Don't rely on people asking first to connect or spending an InMail credit with you. Make it easy by providing the information, and furthermore offering and invitation to call.

It's only when you when you start building a relationship that the real magic of LinkedIn happens. The sooner you can pick up the phone or meet someone, the better.

Take the time to consider your audience and how they might feel buying your product. If it is something that might expose them further to their problem they may not feel comfortable calling during the day or calling at all until they are sure they trust you.

Consider what is happening to them and what step they might like to take next. Pointing to a mailing list, articles, a download or videos might be your best solution for creating meaningful engagement. A really powerful tool is to offer a compelling Call-To-Action that provides a context to a conversation and framework they will feel comfortable in.

Be sure to carefully consider your marketplace and what is going on for them at the time of searching for a provider, or spotting they have a need from your profile.

Of course, these types of invitations are included within your Summary and Experience section, not the official Contact Section, but remember until someone is connected with you, depending on your settings, they will not be able to see your contact details.

In the 2017 updates, the Contact Details were moved to the right-hand-side of the profile on the back layer making them less prominent and hard to see. They also switch places frequently and require a drop down, so let's not rely on people being able actually to find them.

Contact and Personal Info

Jevonte's Profile

Show more ∨

Email

Including your email is important as it gives people the opportunity to send you a personalised message off the platform. If a person doesn't check LinkedIn frequently, or you don't login regularly, email allows you to still make contact and get in front of them fast. Just as we mentioned about jumping on the phone, an email is an even easier and timely way to make contact, so make sure you provide it clearly on your profile.

Before you do though, there is one thing to consider. Your email address reflects the professionalism of your company and your LinkedIn profile. If you use a Yahoo, Google or Hotmail address visitors to your profile will either consider it to be your personal address and avoid emailing, for fear on intruding on your personal time with a work enquiry, or view your company as less established.

As business owners, we need to make the right first impression by having an email address that matches our URL. Such as Naomi@TheProfile.Company for The Profile Company. Make sure to create one and add it as your Primary Email address.

LinkedIn allows you to add multiple emails to your account, which is really necessary if you want people from all areas of your life to find you on one LinkedIn profile. However, you only have to reveal one email address, the one you set as Primary.

Make sure the one you set is your branded email and one you check regularly.

HOW: Changing Your Email Address

The email address shown will be your primary address. To set this or add your company address,

1. Go to the thumbnail photo at the top right of the page. From the dropdown box that appears click 'Privacy and Settings.'

2. Within Basics, you will see Email Addresses listed first.

3. Add in each email address associated with you.

4. Once set, click 'Make Primary' for the one you want to show publicly. You will need to verify your emails first.

TIP: Add All Your Email Addresses to Your Account

Add all the active email addresses you own and currently use from all areas of your life, as doing so will ensure that the right LinkedIn profile appears. If the email is not connected to any LinkedIn account, it will ask the person to invite you to LinkedIn, which since you are already there, is not helpful. Adding all addresses avoids this and enables them to find you.

Websites

LinkedIn allows you to add three websites to your profile. This may feel limited, but actually it keeps things pretty slick and clever. The key thing to remember here is that your profile is designed to capture interest and lead a person seamlessly through your sales funnel. For this to work, we don't need lots of options, as too many will confuse the prospect and lead to inaction.

What we want are three carefully thought-out pages that draw the prospect into the message further and answers their most immediate questions. Note I said 'immediate.' To get this right we need to think about what the prospect has just read on your profile, what they will be curious about and the question they want to be answered right away, and then answer it.

Failure to do so will lead our prospect to turn their curiosity into a Google search and end up on your competitor's website.

Take the time to think what pages you currently have available on your website and where you want prospects to go next. If you have lots of time, you might consider creating custom landing pages that continues the conversation started on LinkedIn with a particular message or video that acknowledges the route they have taken to find you, of course, you wouldn't want it accessible from any other route. Remember this is only an advanced option.

You might consider including a list of your services, portfolio or your blog. Avoid 'About Me' pages since your profile is about you.

LinkedIn's new updates have made website URLs extremely ugly by revealing the full link and placing the Title in brackets. Something that has never been since the invention of the internet! But we have to live with it.

When creating the link try to make it as short as possible and if possible, use 'Pretty Links' to create URLs that are descriptive. Avoid long addresses that scroll over several lines and numbers and letters such as bit.ly/1234si which don't say much or might have people question if it might give them a virus.

Dawn Gregory   ✕

Contact Info

in **Dawn's Profile**
     linkedin.com/in/dawnagregory

∂ **Websites**
     dawngregory.co.uk (Confidence Coaching)

     speakfromtheheart.co.uk/ (Speak from the heart)

     theconfidentspeaker.co.uk (The Confident Speaker)

📞 **Phone**

✉ **Email**

🐦 **Twitter**
     dawngreg59

👥 **Connected**
     December 20, 2016

PrettyLinks is a plugin for Wordpress that allows you to shorten URL to anything of your choice and point to a specific page.

When creating your Titles (the words in brackets) consider carefully what you would like to put here.

By labelling your links with a good title you'll be helping your visitor deciding whether the link worth opening and if they are going to.

People don't click on links that could distract them or lead them down a rabbit hole, so the more confidence you can give by labelling well the better.

LinkedIn offers several options for labelling including stock options and creating your own.

They include Personal, Company, Blog, RSS Feed, and Portfolio.

HOW: Customising Your Website Links

1. Click in on the blue pencil next to your Contact Information.

Contact and Personal Info

in **Your Profile**

2. In the pop-up box that appears, add your website URL.

Edit contact info	Personal	×
	Company	
	Blog	
Website URL	RSS Feed	
	Portfolio	
http://www.theprofile.company/resources-public/	✓ Other	
Type (Other)		
Helpful Resources		
	Remove website	

3. In the second box, label how you want the website to appear.

4. If you select 'Other' a new box will appear below in which you can add your title.

5. Click **Save**.

N.B. Website titles are limited to 30 characters.

Telephone Number

As with your email address, providing your phone number makes it easy for people to get in touch. Including it or not, could be the difference between winning a new contract or it going to someone else.

Including your phone number is entirely your choice. However, if it is available on your website, it really should be on your profile. Making prospects search for the number adds another step that may frustrate your prospect or have them get distracted.

You may opt to include your mobile or just your office number. Within the Contact Information section, you only have room for one number, and it only appears for people who are connected with you (depending on your settings). So you might choose to have your office number in the summary and your mobile only for those who are connections.

For security reasons, it is not a good idea to give away your personal mobile phone number. I'd advise caution here and provide the company number, or consider hiring a call-answering company or have a Skype number that re-routes to your phone.

Skype

Your Skype ID is good to include for first-degree connections if you regularly handle appointments on Skype with new contacts. Scramblling around trying to find someone's Skype address in various messages wastes time, but placing it on your profile will make it an easy reference point for contacts to pick locate it.

One point of note, however, Skype suffers from the same (if not worse) problem as LinkedIn. Cryptic ID names make it hard to identify who is contacting you, and few introduce themselves when they ask to connect, making it unlikely you'll accept the connection. So while it's nice to provide, it is probably going to provide you with little value if you rarely meet with prospects via Skype. Consider carefully.

Twitter

Twitter is great to include if you regularly tweet and people can engage with you that way on a daily basis. However, if you're not a regular user and have few followers, it's best not to include it as it can detract dramatically from the brand image you're working hard to establish. If you don't include it, few will notice, so don't feel any pressure, especially if it's not a profitable strategy for your business.

Avoid using a website URL for your Twitter handle as it can look strange and, as it has its own section, wastes a vital space.

Physical Address

Including your physical address can provide some interesting advantages. Although it isn't necessary, doing so can add a degree of professionalism and a sense of accessibility. Of course, as with all things in branding, this is subjective, so again you'll want to consider the image you wish to convey for your business by ensuring you add a professional address.

EXAMPLE: Your Headline Brings You Gifts

Beyond vanity, of course, there are often very practical reasons for including your business or mailing address. Bert Verdonck, a keynote speaker, frequently receives thank-you gifts in the post because he puts his address on his profile. Plus, as he adds something personal in his headline ('Happy Chocoholic') – so there are no prizes for guessing what he receives!

---

5 Your Profile URL

Each profile has a uniform resource locator (URL), which links directly to your profile. This allows you to connect your website, email signature or other hyperlinks directly to your profile. It also allows you to add it to your business cards so people can easily find you without having to use the search options.

The only issue is the URL given at the time you create your profile is pretty ugly with lots of numbers and letters after your name. Adding this to your business card is unsightly not to mention hard for the person to actually type in.

Thus we need to customise it.

You can find your URL in your browser address bar or within the Contact Information section on the right of the profile. If you want to share with someone just copy paste it as with other things.

When editing your link, it is important to use your full name as it is a vital part of your keyword optimisation. If you have a popular name, it'll likely be too late to not require extra characters on end. As you can see from mine, I have opted to have the UK at the end. Personally, I would avoid keywords specific to your profession to avoid needing to change it if you change jobs, careers or business name as this could prove limiting later.

How: Customising Your LinkedIn URL

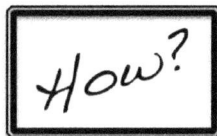

1. Open your Contact Information on the right side of the profile.

2. Click on your URL in blue.

Edit contact info

Profile URL

linkedin.com/in/naomijohnsonuk ↗

3. On the right-hand side, you will see the option to edit your public profile. U

Edit public profile URL

Enhance your personal brand by creating a custom URL for your LinkedIn public profile.

www.linkedin.com/in/naomijohnsonuk ✎

4. Click on the Blue Pencil.

Edit public profile URL

Enhance your personal brand by creating a custom URL for your LinkedIn public profile.

www.linkedin.com/in/naomijohnsonuk

[Save] [Cancel]

Note: Your custom URL must contain 5-30 letters or numbers. Please do not use spaces, symbols, or special characters.

5. You will now be able to edit your URL. If the option you select is not available a red warning message will appear on your screen. Note once you begin editing the URL you will not be able to use any hyphens only letters or numbers with no symbols, spaces or special characters.

Multi-language

LinkedIn gives you the ability to set your profile in multiple languages. If you trade with countries that do not speak your first language, this is an excellent item to include as you'll be speaking to your key audience in a way they can understand. For many

European countries, English is a shared language that most can understand; so having your profile in English as well means that you can easily communicate across borders.

When completing this, it is again worth coming back to the key question we asked at the beginning: What does this person need to know about me to be interested? The answer might differ from country to country, so taking the time to consider your message and any cultural differences. Do not reply to Google to translate but hire a professional with experience of the country, the language, and the culture.

HOW: Creating Multiple-Language Profiles

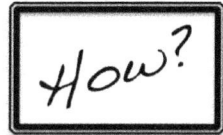

To create your profile in another language,

1. View your profile

2. Locate 'Add profile in another Language' on the right-hand side.

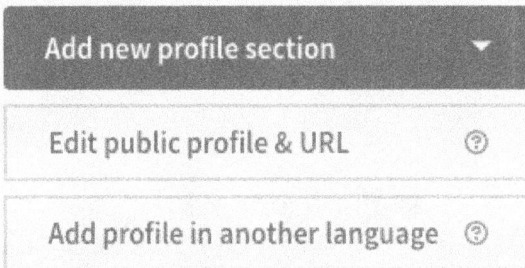

Add new profile section ▼

Edit public profile & URL ⊘

Add profile in another language ⊘

3. Choose a language from the dropdown list and update your first name and last name if they're different in the new profile's language.

4. Translate your existing **Professional Headline**.

5. Translations are not done for you. You need to translate your personal content on your own.

6. Click **Create Profile** to go to the **Edit Profile** page of your new-language profile.

7. Click any **Edit** icon and translate the open fields.

8. Click **Save** and continue editing other sections. *(LinkedIn Help as of April 2017)*

6. Intermediate

Having completed the basics, it's now time to start putting the real grit into your profile. As we've discussed, your objective is to make people stop, read your profile, and take action whether that is learning more about you, telling others about you, or simply learning something important.

At this point, you should know whom your target market is, the keywords associated with it, the steps you want prospects to take as a result of coming to your LinkedIn profile and the unique value you offer.

If you are unsure of these things I recommend reading my book The Expert Economy and completing my online course. It will walk you through each of these elements and help you create a cohesive business plan for growing your business and establishing your personal brand.

www.TheExpertEconomy.co.uk/Book

As we know, people buy from people, and they want to buy from people they know, like and trust. By positioning yourself as a 'go to' expert and focusing on building strong relationships with your prospects, you'll be able to decommoditise your services and have people opt to work with you even if your prices are slightly (or even a great deal) more than a similar business down the road. The key is building the trust with your prospect so there they won't want to go to anyone else.

To do this, we have to pitch your services and your expertise perfectly. One of the fastest ways to do this on your profile is to share a little insight into what you believe, taking the conversation deeper the normal written communication and similar to how you might speak at a networking event.

The most powerful sentences you can use include 'I believe' 'In my opinion' 'I've seen first hand.'

In this section, we delve into each of the different fields available on your profile and discuss how best to complete them in line with your strategy.

> *People buy from people they*
> *know, like, and trust.*

Headline

6

The headline is the text that appears right below your name, and the first thing a visitor reads to understand what you're about. LinkedIn's search function and Google, Yahoo, and Bing pick up the words used in your headline. Therefore, what you include is very important. You might wish to use a full sentence and keywords associated with your industry and the problem you solve.

Since LinkedIn updated in 2017 the format of the headline has changed putting into the debate whether you should have one long sentence that sums up what you do or multiple keywords.

Previous advice was to add something personal about yourself like 'Keen Sailor' or 'Latin Dancer' as this gave a deeper insight into your personality and built rapport, how with the new format you might was to consider whether including this detracts from your key sentence and looks cluttered. Personally, I would always opt for a clean and fresh look that packs a punch.

It is not necessary to include your job title within your headline as it appears directly below anyway. LinkedIn will prompt you to update your headline when you add a new line in your Experience, but avoid saying yes as this will overwrite your manual entry.

Your headline is vital retail space and one of the most important parts of your profile so you'll want to think carefully about it. But don't panic. It can be changed simply enough, and you might like to test out various headlines until you find one you want to settle on.

Headlines can take a little work to get right, but they're well worth the time. When looking at profiles, observe what grabs your attention, what bores you, and which ones make you instantly feel a connection to the person. Remember, your headline needs to grab people's attention with what's relevant to them, so they carry on reading.

EXAMPLE: Crafting Your Headline

Here are some examples, though if you look them up now, they will likely have changed:

Naomi Johnson
Expert LinkedIn Profile Writer | How to Get Leads & What to Do With Them
Portsmouth, United Kingdom

This headline is designed to speak of the problem I solve for people, so if someone is dealing with this issue or looking for my services, they will know to read on.

Dominic Elton 1st
Specialists in Online Video Production | Animation | Music Production | Optimise New Business Opportunities with Video
Drayton, Portsmouth, United Kingdom | Media Production

Using the right keywords, Dominic brought his profile alive with a statement about what his work does.

Sue Carroll

Corporate Reception & IIP Specialist I Creating lasting impressions that reflect the heart and soul of your organization

United Kingdom | Facilities Services

Sue lets organisations know that not only does she specialise in Corporate Reception but that her approach is centered on creating a guest experience that reflects the very heart of the business. By openly stating this in the headline Sue will draw attention away from those with standard headlines and create curiosity. Immediately she has stated that she is a different and the depth her work goes to.

Dilip Shah (K)

Principal Health Consultant ▶ Assisting individuals/corporates seeking cost-effective medical insurance cover worldwide

Pinner, Greater London, United Kingdom | Health, Wellness and Fitness

Dilip quickly states his job title, which puts him in context, and then tells us what his role is. From his job title, not everyone will understand his mission and what he's looking to do, so this is a great way to draw the attention of those looking for assistance.

Exercise: Writing Your Headline

1. What are the keywords associated with your industry and what you do?

2. In one sentence, can you sum up the problem you solve and the value you bring (e.g., How to Get Leads and What to Do with Them)?

3. What are some of your key roles that you want people to know about you?

Experience

7

The experience section is an essential part of your profile as it lets people find out more about you and how you are qualified to help them.

Beyond featuring the logo of the companies you have worked for along with your own, you also have the chance to tell people about your accomplishments during this role. It can be tempting just to add content from your CV and talk about the functional role you played, or list key achievements, but it is in this section we have to be clever.

Remember, your audience aren't recruiters, so don't write for them. Your audience is your friends, family, colleague and those you meet at networking. They don't want to relate you to keywords, but in real terms.

When writing the experience section of your profile, focus on telling the story of your accomplishment. Set the context by outlining what the company did and even the economic climate at that time if it is relevant.

When writing always have your outcome at the front of your mind. Ask yourself 'What does my prospect need to know about me to want to work with me?' What do they need to see in order to understand that you truly are experienced in this and that you are their expert?

For most people consultants, coaches and freelancers, they have a unique take on their industry and the way things should be done. If this is you, take the time to look back over your career and plot the key moments that formed your opinions and created the pivots. Then in the appropriate entry in the experience tell us about it. What did you learn, what did you experience, what did this lead you to believe? Of course, you'll need to write carefully as you should never imply anything negative or inflammatory about anyone else or their company.

Discover Your Value

On The Expert Economy course we have an exercise that will help you uncover the moments and realities that have shaped your thinking and created your expertise.

Go to: www.TheExpertEconomy.co.uk

All too frequently, it can be easy to look back at your past and discredit something you have done as not relevant when it is the one thing that makes you the perfect fit for the role at hand. Take the time to really look.

EXAMPLE: When Your Past Experience Is a Defining Factor

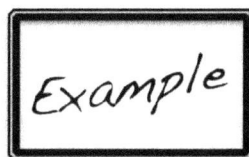

Interviewing David before providing feedback on his profile, I asked him why he had included in his headline 'Business Coaching with the Precision of a Michelin-Star Chef.' When I'd originally read his profile, I couldn't see any reference to his being a chef and had no idea why the statement was relevant. I found out that 20 years prior, he had been a Michelin-star chef. He had chosen not to include it in his profile because he felt it was irrelevant. I encouraged him to put it back on as our experience is what defines us and makes us qualified to do what we do now.

It turned out David had been waiting to hear back from a prospect as to whether he'd be selected to be the key coach for a company. The deciding panel had three executive coaches to choose from and couldn't make up their mind whom to go with. As a last-ditch attempt to choose, they decided to look at the candidates' LinkedIn profiles.

After looking at his profile, now with the update, they instantly selected David as their coach, and now they were 10 times more excited about working with him than before. Why? Because they were a restaurant aspiring for Michelin-star status! Until that point, they had no idea of his previous experience, and had they known; he would have been hired on the spot.

Example

EXAMPLE: When a Lack of Experience Can Hurt You

Of course, your lack of experience could also work against you. One gentleman, I spoke to had chosen to niche his business into one specific industry through his business could work in any.

Reading his profile, I saw no experience listed showing he had a background or connections in this industry. When I asked him, it turned out he'd chosen a niche for his business only because he heard in a business seminar that you need to niche and he had chosen the industry at random.

For his audience, this was never going to work. As people buy from people, in a closed industry, word-of-mouth recommendations are important. Having inroads into a niche area is essential to be able to leverage trust and open doors of opportunity.

For someone seeking to work with a coach, hiring someone with a working knowledge and understanding of the industry is an added advantage for them, though not necessarily essential. By niching, he was making his specialism, his focus, and his pitch on what he could bring to the industry, though he had no experience to back him up. In this instance, he was in the wrong niche. All his profile did was draw attention to how misplaced he was in his niche.

Your LinkedIn profile tells your story whether you've written it with the intention or not. Make sure you craft your message carefully.

People do have a limited attention span so there is no saying how many people will read all of your experience in detail, but you need to include it in case the person is in the final throws of deciding to work with you and reviewing your credentials.

If you are an Author, Business Coach or Success Guru that refers to your past experience frequently, presenting your history in chronological order will add to your position as your audience will be able to identify exactly where and what you were referring to. It will also help them to gain a full understanding of your history and what you have achieved. It provides a level of transparency that shouldn't be overlooked.

A profile shouldn't be filled in like a CV, and you don't have to explain career gaps, missing dates or even jobs that don't fit your personal brand or message. Your profile is yours to do as you wish, though it needs to be accurate and honest. If someone wants to know the omitted information they can ask for your CV.

Your profile is your personal brand. As people have limited attention spans, include the most relevant information and leave out any experiences that might detract from your message.

Remember that the visual representation of your profile is extremely important for a first impression. Having equal length entries is a nice touch and creates the impression of a professional and well-balanced profile.

With the 2017 changes, LinkedIn shortened the Experience section collapsing it with a 'See more' option. This definitely has its merits, but it also means if you have multiple entries for one company, previous work experience can easily be lost.

For one of my clients, he had seven entries for Shell and the two for Kellogg's were lost behind the 'See more' option. His work at Kellogg's is a vital part of his story and this message today, so we didn't want it to be lost behind the 'see more.' Added writing a short paragraph for seven entries felt like overkill. Instead, we opted to collapse all of his experience at Shell into one entry and collapse Kellogg's into one entry, creating an easy read that wasn't over the top.

How far back should your experience go?

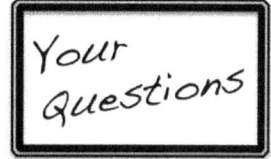

Your Questions

As far back as is appropriate is the general rule. As we saw for David, his Michelin chef experience was 20 years before and in another industry, yet it was the defining factor for him. Some people fear that going way back will age them. This is entirely up to you. If you have relevant experience that could open doors for you, it's your choice whether or not you include it.

Should I include everything?

No.

If you worked in a café or a pub when you were in college, it's not appropriate to include it unless a job or contract you are applying for today requires you to have experience in that area. Even if the experience wasn't a long time ago, you still may not want to include it.

What if I've made a dramatic career change?

The general rule is to include all experience. If you have had a dramatic change in your career, this is part of your story and needs to be included. A profile that only lists one entry raises questions about what you were doing previously and why you aren't disclosing it. Even if someone doesn't consider it as shady, they may feel that it is harder to feel like they understand you and your relevance to what you offer now.

In most cases a dramatic career change is part of your story and why you are qualified to do what you do now. It's your reason why. Thus we want to include it. Use the last entry for your old career to outline why you chose to change direction. Again, remember to keep it positive and anti-inflammatory.

If there is a big reason why you changed, adding a line to your summary might be worthwhile, especially in the early days of your new career. Later, when you have enough time behind you, you might want to remove it from your summary. With limited characters and visitor attention span, you'll need to pitch it well with few words.

Should I list all my freelance jobs?

The answer to this is no because if you had an individual entry for each the profile could get very long. Instead, consider using the Project section of the profile.

Also, avoid feeling the need to complete an up to date list of clients and projects in the

Experience entry. The entry should be about how you help people and how people get work with you, not about your credentials. If you feel it necessary you might open another open position in the Experience section and use this for historic information that your prospect may find helpful.

I did this for a client recently who worked for two companies in a self-employed capacity. Having now opened his own company that delivers the same services, these companies are now his clients. We added them as an entry for before he formalised the company and as a reference point to the clients, and the story they tell about his results.

The key is to continually question how something affects your personal brand and how it will leave your prospect feeling.

Will it leave them feeling confident in you or questioning you? Does it make people question who you are, what you stand for, and your commitment to your industry?

EXAMPLE: Experiences outside Your Profession

Back in 2012, in the middle of my current career, I took two jobs for six months each in

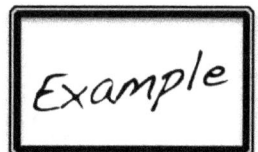

Example

unrelated industries to gain valuable experience and insight that I felt I needed.

While they served my professional development and made sense to me, including them in my LinkedIn profile would create confusion to an onlooker whose sole aim is to get a clear picture of who I am and what I stand for.

Without time to explain my story to them or space to justify why I took those position within in my summary, it is better for me just to leave them out altogether. If it becomes important during a sales conversation, I can explain it to the interested person face-to-face. I have nothing to hide. I just don't want to confuse visitors or risk distracting them from my core message.

Completing the Experience Section

When building the Experience Section of your profile, there are several approaches to consider. If you are self-employed, a business owner or freelancer, the key question an interested visitor will have is 'how can I work with you?' To hold your visitors' attention and convert them into a solid prospect we need to answer them by painting a very clear picture that enables them to see themselves working with you. We need to make your product and services tangible.

Failure to do so will likely lead your prospect to click away from your profile deciding that they aren't that interested anyway, or click through to your website to hopefully find the answer. If it isn't immediately apparent, viewers may again decide it is too much effort and start another task.

If we have the prospect that is now aware they have a problem and curious what investing in a solution now looks like, we want to answer them.

We can't rely on a person picking up the phone to ask. Remember people try to avoid awkward conversations that might embarrass them so they are unlikely to call if there is a chance you will turn them away for something that should have been obvious.

In the Experience entry for your experience, we want to outline how you help clients. Ideally, you want to sum the company up in one short paragraph that leaves no doubt about what you do, the problem you solve, and who you help. In the second paragraph, if space allows you might want to add your belief/mission statement.

Next, we want to outline your packages followed by a strong call to action.

If you have the developed a Product Ecosystem, you'll start with your Product for Clients, Core Product and finish with your Gift for Prospects, since your gift is also your call to action. We take this approach because the Product for Prospects is a lower price, introductory level service and our starting point with clients. Our Core Product is our big-ticket item designed to provide a transformational experience.

With the final item being the free gift, your call to action, you want to pitch the value of having a diagnostic discovery call with you and how to book one. Although people may not take it up at first, they'll have a good sense of how they can interact with you and begin to consider it.

Product Ecosystems

If you haven't yet created a clear product ecosystem, or are unsure what one is, visit www.TheExpertEconomy.com to find out.

This entry is extremely important as it transforms a 'nice idea' into something tangible that people can see themselves actually doing. It gives them something to consider.

In my opinion, unless you are actively looking for a job, the Experience entry for the role you are currently in should pitch your business services, since this is how, in a professional context, you want people to engage with you. It is what you are marketing.

For other entries in the Experience section include things that will matter to your prospect — such as increasing efficiency, reducing costs, and increasing profit. For example, if you handled a crisis and helped overcome it, detail what happened and how you solved it. You may wish to put this in context and say, 'During the economic downturn in 2008, we experienced...And I, working with my team, achieved...' (Remember to be humble here and give credit where it is due as this is a public declaration, and if it's not accurate, it could lead to nasty fallout).

Where possible, use percentages and numbers to help ground the experience and give it more tangibility. Use language and key measurements appropriate to the industry of your target audience.

N.B. If you are a job seeker looking to be hired in a functional role, detailing your responsibilities will be adequate. After all, that's what you're selling—your ability to complete tasks.

TIP: Put Your Results in Context

If necessary, avoid using figures unless you can put them in context. I once had a client

call me to tell me I'd missed 'k' off my profile. I had written that I'd raised £275 at a black-tie ball, and she assumed it should read '£275k' (£275,000). It was embarrassing for both of us when I told her the ticket price was just £12 a head, and thus it was correct. What had been a big win for me at the time, was now peanuts in contrast to the playing field I was operating in. It was better for me not to include the figures at all.

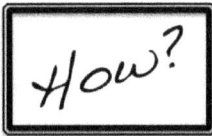
How?

HOW: Writing The Experience Entry for Past Jobs

For a well-structured profile that hits the mark, aim to complete each item in your experience as follows:

1. Company overview (context).
2. Your role.
3. Your results.
4. Insights and key learning that demonstrate what you do now.

If you are completing a description for a job you have now left, visit the website to find how they describe the company and copy/paste the text you find. They'll thank you for it, as you'll be describing the company the way they wish to be.

HOW: Writing the Experience Entry for your Current Role

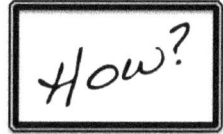

Here we want to tell the prospect exactly what you are up to and how they can engage with you.

1. Summarise what the company does and who its serves.

2. Outline each product in your ecosystem, ideally using Capital Letters for headings, so they stand out.

3. Ensure you include a call to action that directs your prospect to the next stage of working with you.

HOW: Upload Your Experience

1. Visit your own profile.

2. Click the blue + at the top of the Experience Section.

3. Complete each section and indicate if you wish to update your network.

NB. Re-ordering the profile has become very tricky. Only entries that are current open (i.e. Date – Present) can be re-ordered. To do so locate the three horizontal blue lines

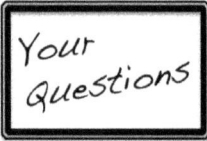

Your Questions

What to Do with Multiple Open Roles

If you have a number of open positions, it's OK to have them all listed as current positions. You will want to consider your personal brand, however, and the main action you want a person to take as a result of coming to your profile.

Come back to the questions:

- What do I most want to be known for?

- What is the most important thing I want people to know?

Adding an entry for your new position at the local Chamber of Commerce is nice to have, but it should go ahead of your core business and marketing message. Thus you'll want to re-order the items.

If you have two roles that are of equal interest, consider the one you most want to lead with, or switch them around as you run different campaigns and each one takes a higher priority in your life.

If you are an author and choose to add an entry in Experience for your book, keeping the position open is important if you want it to be listed high on the profile and not chronologically.

However be sure to consider what you are adding to the profile and how you are explaining it. If you have lots of businesses, you don't want to be seen as someone with too many fingers in too many pies. This is the part where the Summary really comes into play as it allows you to tie the story together.

EXAMPLE: Ensure You Communicate Where Your Priorities Lie

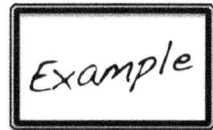

Example

I was recently referred to a company that was struggling to find new recruits. Looking at their employees' profiles, I could see why. Firstly, there was no consistent branding on the profiles, and the company page had recently been started without much thought or planning. Secondly, the managing director had two open positions in his experience and no summary. Why is this a problem? Because for the onlooker it seems as though the MD has multiple interests and is not committed to the company.

A well-thought, thorough summary, however, would easily overcome this, detailing how the two are related and, most likely, showing the company to be a dynamic and exciting mover in the industry.

TIP: Demonstrate Your Experience

Each item of experience also comes with the capability to add rich content media, so you have the opportunity to add slides, videos, and PDFs related to the position that can contribute towards creating a fuller picture of who you are, what you've done, and what you've achieved.

I always say to add a minimum of two items so that the profile looks balanced and well thought out. Again consider the message of each item and what you are trying to convey to the reader.

8

Your Summary

Your Summary is your chance to overcome many of the issues that may have arisen writing your Experience. If you do have multiple interests or positions, now is the time to sow them together and have them make sense.

With the 2017 updates, the Summary has now been collapsed to two lines followed by 'see more.' However, don't think that the section is now lost. It will still be seen, especially since it will remain in an expanded view for your visitor for several more views.

Of course, those first two lines are now more important than ever.

The key to a good summary, as with the rest of your profile, is to consider your audience and what they most need to know about you to be interested. Your objective should be to leave them feeling excited, intrigued, and eager to know more.

What does your audience most need to know about you to be interested?

Ideally, we want to take a person through each stage of the Buying Cycle (see page 72) within the 2000 characters including spaces available. This might sound like a big ask, but it can be done with skill.

As space is limited, we don't want to include information that is already available elsewhere and isn't relevant the main message of your profile.

Instead, we want to begin by setting the context for the conversation we're about to have with our prospect, i.e. create awareness.

By outlining the problem, we solve our visitor will not only quickly grasp the context of the conversation but also be intrigued. A well-written paragraph will inform the prospect and tell them something they didn't know.

The idea is, that even if they aren't our ideal prospect and will never buy from us, that we leave them with an interesting nugget of information that they remember it and tell others. This creates awareness in the marketplace on our behalf. It might sound strange to say such a thing, but we aren't we always looking for interesting things to add to conversations or offer up at dinner parties? Think of your opening paragraph in this context. What is an interesting fact that people will remember and want to talk about relevant to the problem you solve?

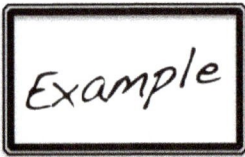

Example

EXAMPLE: Educate Your Audience with a Punchy Opening

Skip Archimedes promotes health and well-being, a very populated market. Most people, unless diagnosed with a problem, probably think they are doing OK health wise and just carry on living life never realising they are living below their full potential. Bring a person to a realisation on this and getting them to take action a real challenge.

In Skip's profile we grab people's attention with some hard-hitting facts before stating his mission to bring change; a mission that others can understand and go along with. But who is he and why should we follow him? In the next part of his summary we outline his background; what has happened to him, what he has overcome and why he is qualified to help.

With limited space on the summary (2000 characters including spaces), we wanted to sum up his information and use the Website quickly. So, we provided links in the 'About Me' information should people want to learn more.

In todays world the first sign of a heart attack is the heart attack. For the first time ever, it is predicted that parents will out live their children. Fertility is on the decrease as miscarriages are on the increase. And our farming choices have led to our fruits and vegetables to contain just 5-20% of the nutritional value they did 100 years ago.

Our current way of life has weakened our gene pool and it is simply unsustainable.

And I am on a mission to change this!

Having overcome serious illnesses as a child, a family breakup, obesity, depression, and recovered from a broken back after Doctors told me I'd never walk again, I know personally what it takes to make a choice to transform your life.

On my retreats (Detox Your Life & Breakthrough Mastery), my clients achieve life changing results guaranteed, because what I teach works. And this is why people call me the Miracle Man.

Most people are living below capacity, completely unaware that there is more to life than feeling tired, sluggish, popping pills and fighting acid reflex as a normal part of life – in fact on my courses, we can rid you of acid reflex permanently in just one day!

If you're sick of living below your capacity, and curious to explore your potential, then I invite you to spend the weekend with me - at my expense - with a free ticket to my 2-day Supercharge Your Life event.

But don't take my word for it! See what my clients have to say with the testimonials below!

I have a wide range of resources to help you in your journey to health that I hope you'll allow me to share with you. It is my desire to see everyone LIVE STRONG, LIVE HEALTHY and LIVE LONG!

HOW: Writing Your Profile as a 'Go To' Expert and Industry Thought Leader

When writing your profile refers to the diagram 'How people buy' and structure each paragraph accordingly.

The follow paragraph structure is just a suggestion, but the principles are all there.

1. Outline the facts and concerns surrounding the problem you solve (create awareness).
2. Outline what your company does and your mission within your business related to this problem (invest).

3. Provide your background story as to why you are qualified to solve it.
4. Outline the services you offer.
5. State the urgency for the problem to be solved.
6. Insert the call to action.

EXAMPLE: Put Things into Perspective

When in recruitment, it's important to give a full overview of the size and scope of the company and not assume people know. As senior vice president of ASDA, Hayley's profile gives a comprehensive overview of the company and lets us know the awards it's won as an employer.

Asda's mission is to be Britain's most trusted retailer, exceeding customer needs every day. We're one of the largest grocers in the UK, with nearly 600 stores and around 200,000 employees. And we've frequently been named one of Britain's best places to work, winning the Top Employer award, Retail Week's Employer of the Year and being placed in The Times newspaper's 'Best Companies To Work For.' Since 1999 we have been part of Walmart, the world's biggest retail company with nearly 11,000 stores worldwide.

This information won't be relevant to all members of the team but remember it's all about the outcome that you want.

For Clive, the key information he needs to convey is the value his department provides for Canon's channel partners. Thus, his opening statement is a quick and straight-to-the-point overview of what the company does.

Canon is a world-leading innovator and provider of imaging and information technology solutions or home and office environments. At Canon, we pride ourselves on quality of our products and services, our relationships and our partners. It is this that drives our success.

How?

HOW: Writing Your Profile Summary if You're Employed

If you're employed and just looking to put a smart profile together, a quick way to create a professional finish is to use this three paragraph structure:

1. Summary of the company.

2. Summary of your role in the company.

3. Something personal about you.

To write about your company visit their website and look for keywords or paragraphs about the company that you can copy/paste. The company has, after all, invested money crafting this text to position the company accurately, so why not use it. With a little tweaking, you can easily make it fit your sentence structure.

Adding something personal about you provides an insight into you as a person that might intrigue a prospect or develop a higher level of rapport.

If you're self-employed, however, you'll not want to use this method.

Write something personal

As I've discussed, the objective of your profile is to connect with your audience in a way that develops familiarity and trust. The more someone feels that they know you, the higher the chance they will like you, and when someone likes you, trust and business follow. Including something personal about yourself helps a person to view you as a three-dimensional person. It helps them develop a rapport with you and feel comfortable.

The best way to achieve this is to create a 'me too' reaction. This is where the person recognises that you do something they do, and says 'me too.' It creates an instant attraction between two people as it gives them something mutual to talk about that isn't business-related. Talking about non-business-related subjects will quickly move you from a 'sales person' to a 'friend' and make a person open up to you. Of course, you want to keep the conversation relevant and interesting, and that is why volunteering information is so valuable. Although your customer does not need to use this information in a conversation with you, you may just find they bring it up as a way to get to know you.

As a service provider and the person reaching out, you'll likely be the person using this information to start a conversation. By providing it on your profile, you're encouraging them to do the same, giving everyone this advantage.

Previously LinkedIn provided a section for including your Interests. This made including this information easier. Now, however, we have to depend on our LinkedIn Summary, or a word or two in our headline, to fit it in.

These days, when writing profiles for people, I don't include it, as there simply isn't space.

Should you feel it important though, you might include your hobbies or a list of your priorities and interests. If you're actively pursuing a sport and actively competing, could prove very fruitful as a conversation starter.

For ideas on what to include, again consider your audience. If you have a very family-orientated clientele, it is worth speaking about your family—e.g., 'On Sunday afternoons, I enjoy hiking with my three children.' What you include quickly demonstrates your values and what's important to you, and if you can make someone laugh, even better.

Anything that gives people an insight into you and your personality is worth including. Remember to tailor it appropriately to your audience and the business environment you're in.

When writing your profile, it is worth consulting with a copywriter, who will be able to help you form your message and see qualities in you and synchronicities in your story you may not have been able to see alone.

If you feel you need help writing it or would just like to get an external perspective, visit www.TheProfile.Company to book a LinkedIn Profile Review. At TheProfile.Company we write profiles for solo-entrepreneurs, sales teams, and business leaders and will be happy to talk to you.

How you write your profile is very important. You'll want to get a sense check from others as to whether you communicate what you think you do. In the hundreds of LinkedIn reviews, I've conducted, the one thing that surprises me the most is how different people's roles or interests are from what they write on their profiles.

Before each session, I take the time to read the person's profile, and then during the session, I ask them to explain what they do spontaneously. The difference is very telling. What I have found is that people write their LinkedIn profiles in professional business language using big words, but when they speak about what they do, often full of passion and interest, they present themselves very differently. They present themselves 'relationally'—i.e., they know they are speaking to individuals and so attempt to create a relationship with them.

For one client I worked with, I reviewed their regular business literature and wasn't very excited. I asked if there was other content anywhere that described what they did. I was referred to an article written about them by a journalist for a major newspaper, and there I found just the description I was looking for. Newspapers are written for audiences they are building a 'relationship' with; thus, the wording and approach in the article were completely different. It was far more engaging, and it created a vivid picture in my mind of what the organisation did and what value it could provide.

TIP: Test your profile

If you choose to write your own profile, it's important to test it with your audience. Often what you think you have said, isn't what you have said, or the language you have used is the language you use internally within the company, but not the language your prospects use. Thus it doesn't resonate with them.

Make sure you use the types of words they use and talk about the symptoms of the problem. Use keywords and terms they frequently use to invoke the response 'this is me' or, for friends and family that surround them 'Is this what Bob complains about? I should forward this to him.

EXAMPLE: When using the wrong language attracts the wrong audience

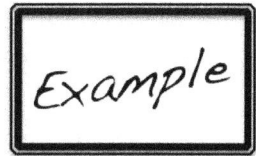

Example

One of our clients had created a successful profile. He knew this by the number of new enquiries coming into his business each week. However, when he took the time to review who the new leads were, he saw a startling trend. Not one of them was his target audience. Further investigation showed that his language was too generic and he was attracting prospects in positions lower than his ideal clients.

In the hundreds of LinkedIn reviews I've conducted, the one thing that surprises me the most is how different people's roles or interests are from what they write on their profiles.

The client revamped his summary, changing his language to use words and key terms found only in the boardroom. As soon as he changed his profile, the types of enquiries changed. Those lower in the organisation were no longer interested, mainly because they couldn't understand what he was saying. If they did understand, they knew that he wasn't a coach for them. His ideal prospects, however, instantly recognised him as someone who understood them and their position. His use of language indicated his skill level immediately, and he became an intriguing option for them.

Example

EXAMPLE: Write for Your Audience

Donna is a seasoned leadership and development trainer who has worked in large organisations. Her services tend to be sought by the HR department. Traditionally, they have required her to submit a full CV/portfolio and still do now. Donna has an excellent reputation for constant employment, so her LinkedIn profile simply backs up her brand and helps her connect with her delegates (each of whom could go on to be a future referrer or contractor of her services).

When crafting Donna's profile, it was important to keep in mind her target audience and stay relevant to them. The purchaser and decision maker for Donna's services is the HR department. Providing the information they require on her LinkedIn profile is the most relevant thing she can do, including attaching her traditional resume to the profile for easy access.

At this stage, Donna doesn't have a particular angle on leadership for which she'd like to be considered as a 'thought leader'. If she had, however, we might have designed her profile differently. For her profile, it was important to make hiring her easy, and that means providing her target audience with the exact information they need. Any additional information might attract time-consuming queries from outside her target market, making LinkedIn more of a hindrance than helpful.

Recommendations

9

Recommendations are an important way of increasing your credibility and your audience's confidence that you can do a job well. LinkedIn prioritises messages from your first-degree connections, so they show first— i.e. your audience will first see testimonials about you from people they know.

As I've emphasised, grabbing and keeping your audience's attention is important, so long-winded, off-the-point testimonials won't get read.

In the 2017 changes, testimonials were detached from the positions they were written for and collected all together in one place. The amount of text show also increased to approximately 600 characters including spaces.

Even though more is now shown beyond the previous 'see more' option, we still need to make sure the testimonial achieves what we want.

But how do we achieve this when we are not the person writing it?

You'd be surprised just how normal it is for people to write their testimonials. If someone has agreed to write one, they are likely to run into two obstacles: they don't know what to say, and they can't find the time to do it.

Once the person has agreed to publish a testimonial for you, you can volunteer to write it for them, giving them final editing permission. Most people will jump at this option as they don't really know what to say.

If they agree you have the ability to structure the testimonial just as you need emphasising what you feel is most important.

One time I needed a letter of recommendation for a new contract writing LinkedIn profiles, so I asked a previous company if they would supply one. The letter

I received back was nice, but it wasn't specific and didn't highlight each stage of the journey. Thus I opted to tweak it adding in details and information to go along with the positive words they had said. When I sent it back to my contact, his response was 'Great. That is everything I would have wanted to say but wouldn't have known how to.'

Another time a friend of mine needed three testimonials urgently. I helped her identify the clients that were best fit, but one of them was met with the comment 'He would never have the time to do that for me, especially not in the next two hours.' To which I responded – yes but I can.

While she jumped on the phone to him to ask his permission, I wrote her a glowing testimonial highlighting all the things her new contract needed to know about working with her and that I knew was true of her service. Thirty minutes later he had approved it, and the testimonials were sent.

Crafting your testimonials is important. They require just as much care as other parts of your profile since if they are boring and add no value, your prospect will simply opt out of reading it before they get to the main part.

A testimonial might be about how your business operates and conducts itself, such as in a cleaning business, or it might be the results you've achieved for your client through your work.

For the latter, a testimonial wants to read something like this:

> 'Prior to working with [name], we were going £100k into the red each month due to a poorly designed production line and frustrated distribution channels. After working with [name], we have seen a 130% increase in efficiency and a 150% increase in profitability. Working with [name] was an absolute pleasure. Everyone in the team, from the CEO to the floor worker, enjoyed working with [name], and he definitely delivers on his promises'.

How?

HOW: Requesting a Testimonial

1. First, ensure you are connected to the person you want to request a testimonial from.

2. Open the profile of the person from whom you wish to request a testimonial.

3. Next, to the blue Connect button, you will see a box with three dots in it. Click on this box.

4. From the drop-down menu, select 'Request a Recommendation'.

Message ···

↪ Share Profile

↓ Save to PDF

⊗ Remove Connection

⊐ Report / Block

✕ Unfollow

▥ Request a Recommendation

▥ Recommend

onal roller coaster and to win you need the very l
king with my team because winning is why we d

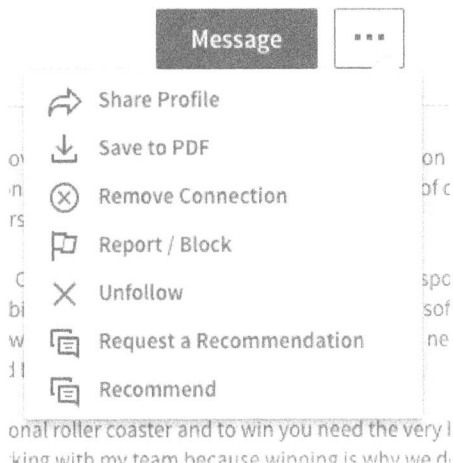

5. The pop-up boxes that appear will help you navigate through each step. You will have the opportunity to select how you knew each other, the role you worked in and write a personalised message with your request.

N.B. If you have already agreed that you will write the testimonial you can put your text into the message. The person will then need to copy/paste it into the right section on their end once ready. You will have the ability to approve and ask for revisions of the recommendation before it is published. You always maintain control of published testimonials.

How?

HOW: Sending a Recommendation

If you would like to send someone a recommendation, simply follow the steps 1-4 in the previous 'how' and select 'Recommend.'

10

Education

This section is absolutely vital to your credibility. If you are professing to be an expert in something but don't have the education to back it up, people will question whether you really know what you're doing. Including it gives people a fuller picture of you and enables them to make a personal connection with you.

If you are setting yourself up as an expert, but you don't have official qualifications, you can counter this by adding in courses and training you have received. The **Courses** section on LinkedIn allows you to provide only the title of the course, so if you want to include more specific information, it is better to use the **Education** section. You can also include videos and slideshows. Completing this section is good because, in addition to your official qualifications in the discipline, it shows your dedication and interest in the subject and your effort to keep your knowledge up-to-date.

If you have not taken any courses and had nothing to write, ensure you tackle this issue well in your **Summary**.

Interestingly, once you've connected your education to the official college/university page, you'll find LinkedIn predicting more relevant connections as it'll start finding your classmates and other alumni, who, due to the nature of these relationships, will have greater affiliation and inclination to help you out and are perhaps some of the most valuable connections in your network.

Publications

11

If you've written a book or had articles published, you'll want to add these to your profile to add to your credibility and give people a chance to spend time with you to discover the depth of your knowledge and your 'take' on the world.

Accomplishments   +

3 Publications   ⌄
   What to Put on Your LinkedIn Profile • The Truth About Starting a Business • Grass Roots to Green
   Shoots

Again Publications was a section that received an overhaul in the 2017 updates that didn't work in favour of published authors. Instead of allowing us to feature our works of blood sweat and tears, they are now collated together with just a number and a further drop down box in the Accomplishments Section.

Of course, you'll want to add all your books here, and potential links to magazine, newspaper and online blogs where you have been featured, however for actual books that make up a part of your credentials and your sales funnel, I recommend a separate entry in your Experience section.

You may like to make an entry for each book or bundle them together under an entry title "Author" with the company name being the books. You can use Rich Content Media to upload slideshows that show the front cover of the book, what the book is about and a link through to where a person can buy it.

Try to avoid just adding the front cover of the book as it will do little to help the person learn about the book, decide whether to buy it and actually get their hands on it.

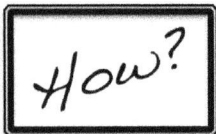

HOW: Adding Publications to Your Profile

If this is your first publication:

1. Visit your profile and click on 'Add a new profile section' in the top right corner.

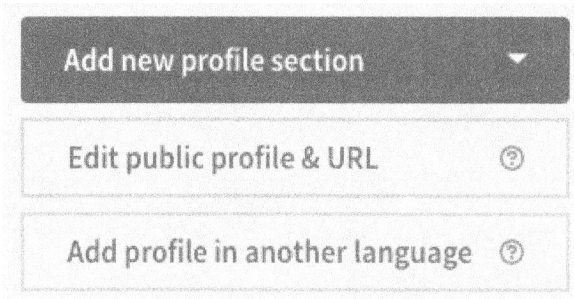

Add new profile section ▼

Edit public profile & URL ⊙

Add profile in another language ⊙

2. The drop-down box that appears has three sections; Background, Skills, Accomplishments. When you select 'Accomplishments' publications will appear in the list of options.

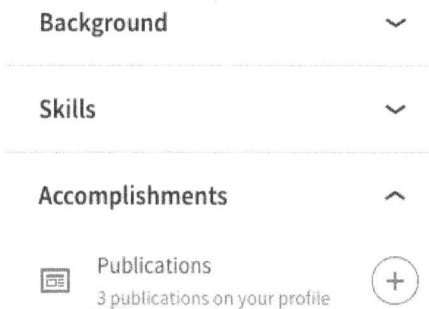

Background ⌄

Skills ⌄

Accomplishments ⌃

Publications
3 publications on your profile (+)

3. Click the + symbol in the circle.

4. A pop-up will appear asking you for the title, the publisher or publication, the date of publication, co-authors, and a URL to the book.

5. For the book URL, include a link to where your publication is hosted, whether that's an online version of the publication or where the person can buy your book, such as Amazon.

TIP: Getting the Most from Your Authorship

Using this option, you won't be able to upload any rich content media, such as a free sample of the book or a SlideShare about it. One option you might take is to add **Author** to your experience and put your content there. Including a few free chapters of your book with a link to where to purchase is a highly effective strategy.

12

Projects

The **Projects** function provides an opportunity to exhibit your work and explore your key messages. You might use it to show past work or draw specific attention to things you are currently working on, such as a new book, a research project, an event, or a fundraising or recruitment drive.

By inviting your team to connect to the project, you are furthering your exposure and thus attraction. You'll want to attach everyone associated to it, so remember to write it for multiple standpoints so it's positioned correctly for each person whose profile it will appear on.

Projects use to have a prominent place but are now captured inside 'Accomplishments', so they don't pull the attention they once did. They are worth including however if they demonstrate your expertise and what you are capable of.

When writing your project be sure to focus on the problem that you solved, rather than just simply saying what you did. Your key audience will be interested in the transformation you delivered (or are intending to deliver), and this starts with outlining the extent of the problem before you started working with them and why you were called in.

Projects are a great alternative to having multiple open roles. If you are a freelancer working with many companies and don't want to clog up your Experience entry, projects allow you to show what you are working on and/or have worked on.

Skills & Endorsements

LinkedIn gives you the opportunity to list your skills and have your connections

13

endorse you, confirming that you have them. Many are not keen on this function as it doesn't provide a true and accurate reflection of your skill set or confirm that the person endorsing you has experienced this skill set from you.

The skills do however contribute towards SEO and thus how often you are found for keywords so paying attention to them is important.

If you are finding you are being endorsed for skills you do not have, or you no longer wish to be known for, you can delete skills and add more relevant ones.

With the new updates only your top three, highest ranked skills will show, so think carefully what you would like these skills to be. Remember there is a lot of other things on your profile contributing to your overall message, so spending time here may not be as worthwhile as investing in other areas of your profile.

How?

HOW: Organising Your Skill Set

Adding New Skills:

1. Visit your LinkedIn profile and locate the skills section.

Entrepreneurship · 99+   Endorsed by Rob Brown and 8 others who are highly skilled at this

Coaching · 99+   Endorsed by Rob Brown and 25 others who are highly skilled at this

                            Endorsed by 2 of Naomi's colleagues at Really Connect

Training   91   Endorsed by Vicky Ross and 9 others who are highly skilled at this

See 19 more skills ﹀

2. To 'Add a new skill' click on the button top right of the section.

3. In the pop-up that appears, begin typing in the skill you would like to add. LinkedIn will start predicting options for you to select. You can opt to select those words or create a new term that isn't on the list.

4. Next, click Add.

Delete or Re-Order Skills:

1. Click on the Blue Pencil.

2. In the pop-up that appears click the x on the left-hand-side to remove skills you do not want.

3. To re-order, hover your mouse over the icon with three lines on the right-hand side. Once you have finished close the pop-up window by clicking save at the bottom of the box.

Skills & Endorsements (22)

Delete	Skill	Reorder
✕	Entrepreneurship · 99+	☰
✕	Coaching · 99+	☰
✕	Training · 91	☰
✕	Strategy · 83	☰
✕	Leadership Devel... · 59	☰
✕	Marketing Strategy · 56	☰
✕	Leadership · 52	☰
✕	Business Develop... · 49	☰
✕	Business Strategy · 46	☰
✕	Social Media Mar... · 37	☰

Manage pending Endorsements

1. If you have a notification for pending endorsements, click on the blue words.

2. In the pop-up box that appears you will have the option to either add the skill to your profile or ignore it.

Endorsements   ✕

Add these new skills to your profile

Business Planning
Endorsed by Zulfiqar Ali   Ignore   [Add to profile]

Marketing
Endorsed by Zulfiqar Ali   Ignore   [Add to profile]

Social Media Communications
Endorsed by Elizabeth Graney   Ignore   [Add to profile]

Determine how you are endorsed:

LinkedIn gives you several options for an endorsement that you can switch on or off as you require.

You can opt to be endorsed, to be included in endorsement suggestions appearing on other people's profiles, and opt to see suggestions for people you might like to endorse.

1. Click on the Blue Pencil in the Endorsement section

2. At the bottom of the list of skills, you will see 'Adjust Endorsement Settings'

3. A pop-up box will appear. Use the slider to select Yes or No for each option.

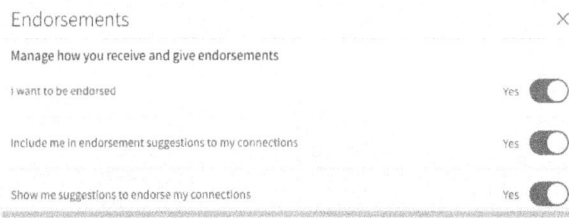

Endorsements	✕
Manage how you receive and give endorsements	
I want to be endorsed	Yes ⬤
Include me in endorsement suggestions to my connections	Yes ⬤
Show me suggestions to endorse my connections	Yes ⬤

Endorsing people is a good way to get noticed however I would advise only endorsing people for skills you know they have and that they want to be known for.

Personally, I don't accept endorsements from people I don't know that have no idea what I am capable of, or people within my close network who endorse me for skills I either don't have or don't want to be known for.

Endorsements are a personal opinion and entirely up to you. Since most people accept endorsements from they don't know, the general population of LinkedIn can't truly put must weight on them. Of course for keyword ranking and being found on the platform, they do have their place.

---

7. Advanced

By now you should have the majority of the elements of your profile in place and be ready to go. The following items are advanced options that will add an extra something to your profile, but they aren't things that should stop you publishing your profile and getting active building your business.

Getting these items right, however, will certainly make your profile stand out from the crowd and support your prospect in their decision-making. So if you do have the time they are worth the investment. You may of course already have these items available on other social media platforms or can easily adapt them from proposals, presentations or reports already sitting on your computer.

Rich Content Media

Within your LinkedIn profile, you have the opportunity to upload what is called 'Rich Content Media.'

Media (3)   ⟨ Previous   Next ⟩

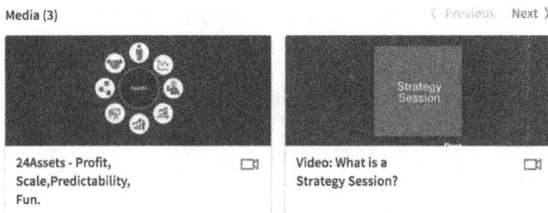

24Assets - Profit,   Video: What is a
Scale,Predictability,   Strategy Session?
Fun.

Rich Content Media are videos, PDFs, and slideshows that can be added to the Summary and Experience Sections of your LinkedIn Profile.

Using them will allow you to share more of your message and take your prospect further through their buying journey and deepen their relationship with you.

There appears to be no limit to how much you can upload per entry at the moment. However you do want to think carefully before throwing everything on there.

Before deciding what to publish on your profile or what to create especially, it's important first to consider your prospect and the journey they are on.

We have spoken about focusing on the problem you solve and bringing prospects to the awareness that, yes they may well have a problem. We have also spoken about helping people diagnose that this is the problem they have and bringing them around to the fact that they need to invest in a solution.

The content we create needs to do a few things. Firstly it needs to help the prospect to identify further and diagnose their problem, and then educate them to the point where they can either solve it for themselves, or they see the value investing in a solution.

We will have started each part of this message within the text on your profile, but there isn't a great deal of room to say everything we might want to. Therefore Rich Content Media is a great option.

We want to create a mixture of formats to match each persons learning style and the environment they are in when viewing our profile. Not everyone has headphones easily available to play a video in a public place.

Each item needs to be compelling and get quickly to the point. No one will stick around, and digest content that they aren't sure is valuable to them or where they are right now.

Therefore what we supply needs to be a natural progression of what we've already talked about on the profile and answer the next logical questions a person will have about working with us or diagnosing their situation further.

Too much content will overload a prospect and confuse them, leading them not to view any of the options we have supplied.

Our goal is to create just the right pieces that will lead our prospect though our sales funnel in a logical way, always adding value to them. A few well thought out pieces of content is all we need.

The only time this advice differs is if you are the host of a podcast or video series. In this instance, you would exhibit the content you have available and allow your prospect to first get a full idea of the types of things you offer and also try out the ones that appeal to them.

Developing Content

The content you create needs to add value and it needs to contain the conversation. This means your profile needs to lead a prospect into your existing sales funnel off LinkedIn (such as a landing page or squeeze page) or it needs to bring people directly back to your LinkedIn profile (by digesting the other items you've supplied on your profile).

Ultimately our goal is to have a profile visitor connect with you motivated to start a conversation about working with you.

To do this, we need to evaluate what you have already said and what someone needs to know further. For example, one of my clients provides an app that helps their prospects explore what they need to migrate their business platforms from one provider to another, including assessing the business needs and how to have internal conversations. It's a comprehensive and vital tool for anyone within his or her market. However that doesn't mean that someone is just going to download it and remember to use it.

Although it is mentioned in the profile and pitched as a valuable tool, we still have work to do.

By using a Slideshare presentation or even a video, we can demonstrate to people exactly what this tool does, giving people the opportunity to see it and evaluate whether it is something they can see themselves using.

Relying on someone to click through to a page from a link on our profile is lazy, especially when links within content are not hyperlinks and require the person to copy paste. For someone to do this, we would have had to pitch exceedingly well.

When we know this and evaluate the likelihood of our prospect doing something we think is obvious, we begin to identify what content we need to be making.

The content we publish might be video footage of an event with testimonials, and introduction video to who we are, a sample chapter of our book, or a slideshare presentation of our services. The options are limitless, yet we need to craft them carefully, so they create a seamless journey for our prospects.

Creating these items doesn't have to be time-consuming or costly. The key is to ensure they answer the most pressing questions of your audience in a way that sets you up as an expert. If you're a small business with little budget, these items can be easily produced with the software already in-built on your computer. It doesn't require anything special. With a little attention, you can produce something of reasonable quality and brand it to your business.

Our goal is to create enough content that someone feels that they've spent time with you and got to know you. This is critical for building rapport and loyalty. A mixture of content that clearly pitches you as the expert and adds value to the prospect, actually helping them move forward, is critical.

"My boss wants me to be using LinkedIn to find new people, but I have absolutely no idea how!"

Webinar: LinkedIn - Productivity Tool or a Time Waster?

Uploading Content

Each item appears in a box with a graphic and caption below. You will have the opportunity to edit the caption below the graphic upon uploading, but no influence over the graphic. This will need to be taken care off before you upload to LinkedIn.

You will have the option to Upload the files directly to LinkedIn or link to content publish on another platform such as YouTube.com, Slideshare.net, etc.

Caption

LinkedIn will automatically populate the description and caption field when uploading. However you will have the opportunity to edit it.

It is worth noting, that making sure you write the description and content correctly during the upload process on your host platform will save you time later, especially if you have other employees or team members who will also use this content as it means the correct message is consistent on all platforms. Plus if someone shares your content, they too will be presenting your best message.

When uploading to LinkedIn include a caption that clearly demonstrates what the content is and why someone should look at it. You might even go as far as writing what type of content it is, like in the example it says 'Video:'

Since the 2017 updates, this isn't altogether necessarily as LinkedIn have added an icon to each item to denote what type of content it is. Thus the choice is yours.

It is vital that people know since they will only click on content appropriate for their environment or their mood. Thus we might opt to create a slideshow version of the same message, so people don't have to watch the video if they don't want to.

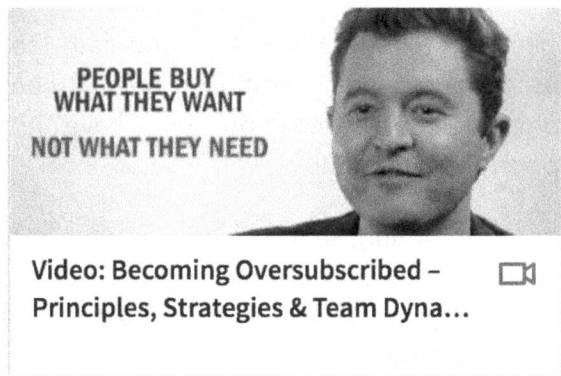

PEOPLE BUY WHAT THEY WANT

NOT WHAT THEY NEED

Video: Becoming Oversubscribed – Principles, Strategies & Team Dyna...

Correct labelling will give your prospect more confidence about what they are about to click on. People are always conscious about what they open on their computers, and what they are allowing to distract them. The better the campaign, the better the caption.

A good caption starts by clearly stating the format that it is in—for example:

Webinar: How to create an engaging profile.

Video: Introduction to CapMania.

FREE: Sample chapters of [book title].

In light of the new changes, you may choose to opt out of adding Webinar or Video before the title.

Creating a Presentation

Before uploading a presentation check first how it will appear on LinkedIn as the viewer isn't always that big. Videos tend to be fine, but some uploaded slideshares and PDFs only get a small window, and therefore, if your presentation has too much text on it, it can be hard to see. We need to make each slide readable considering the viewer. We don't want our prospect to feel frustrated trying to read the content. This might mean we need to add more pages to our presentation and increase the font size until it has the impact that we're looking for.

Remember too that the content is also part of our brand message, so be sure to keep the same tone of voice, consistency of message and most importantly, apply the company branding correctly.

HOW: Uploading Rich Content Media

There are two ways to upload content, either by adding a file or by adding a link. To access either,

1. Click on the blue pencil associated with the item on your profile that you want to add the Rich Content Media too.

2. Within the pop up you will the option for updating all information relating to this position, however, scroll right to the bottom until you see 'Media.'

Media

Add or link to external documents, photos, sites, videos, and presentations.

Upload	Link

⑦ Supported formats

Upload a File:

3. Click on **Upload File**, and you will immediately be able to upload a file directly from your computer.

Add a Link:

4. Copy/paste the link into your media item and click **Continue**.

Upload	Link

Paste or type a link to a file or video   Add

⑦ Supported formats

5. LinkedIn will naturally pull in 160 characters with spaces before cutting off. You can add up to 500 characters however. Note you may have to click out of the window and back again before it tells you that you are over the character count.

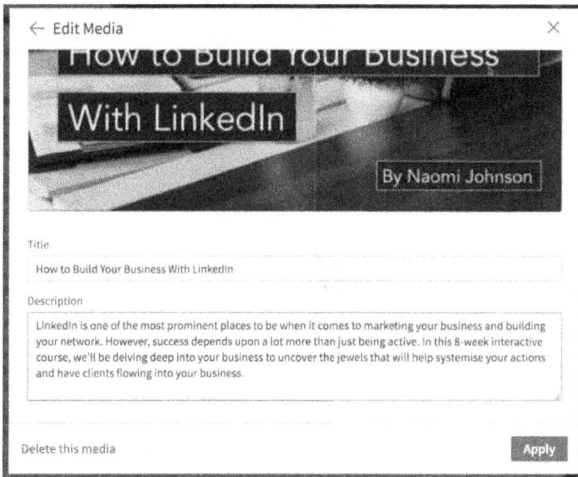

TIP: Ensure the Correct Description Is on the Host site

If you want multiple people to post this item of content, don't leave the description up to them to write or copy/paste. LinkedIn will automatically pull 160 characters from the description from the host site, i.e., where the media was originally uploaded. To avoid inconsistent or wrong information, ensure your description, along with the call to action, is part of the description for the original upload. With only 160 of 500 characters actually being pulled in, you may have to consider sending out an additional text to your team to add into the profile.

Establish the Next Steps

Before crafting your item carefully consider the next step you want your prospect to take. Do you want them to call you or join a mailing list? You will want to know this upfront so you can build it into the presentation, by pitching the value of the next item available and providing a link.

Knowing that your prospect has spent the time with you here and digested the content to this point in the video – where your call to action is inviting them to make the next step – will help you to work out exactly what to offer next. Offering a video within a video is to keep the prospect at the same level of the sales funnel. Instead, you might offer them a download (that requires details to access) or invite them to speak with you directly.

The last thing you'll want to do is invite them to follow you on Facebook since LinkedIn and Facebook are at the same level as each other in the sales funnel. We want to take people further, not backward.

Consider carefully what is the logical next step and 'easy yes' for your prospect to take based on what they have just learned from you and how it has supported them in their buying journey with you.

Formats to Upload

There are a variety of formats you can upload to LinkedIn including:

- Adobe PDF (.pdf).
- Microsoft PowerPoint.
- (.ppt/.pps/.pptx/.ppsx/.pot/.potx).
- Microsoft Word (.doc/.docx/.rtf).
- OpenOffice Presentation Document (.odp).
- OpenOffice Documents (.odt).
- Most .txt files.
- .jpg/.jpeg.
- .png.
- .bmp.
- .gif – this doesn't support animation, however the first frame will be extracted.
- .tiff.

Personally, I always advise not to add .pngs or .jpg as the single item alone adds very little value to the profile. Ideally, we want content that engages our prospect and makes it worth the effort to click on the link and then have to shut it again to return to LinkedIn. If the item was nothing but a photo that they will be disappointed by the extra effort made.

When uploading make sure:
- The file size does not exceed 300 MB.
- The maximum resolution for images is 120 megapixels.

Here are some suggestions for things you might choose to include:

Slideshows

Publishing the slides from a keynote talk or webinar is a great way to engage your audience as people can quickly flick through the slides and read your key information without much commitment. It is a great alternative to a video as there is no sound to disguise if the person is at work or in a public place.

The key to a good slideshow is to use bullet points and avoid long paragraphs. Although this slideshow won't be delivered from the front of the room as it normally would, you still don't want to overload people, so keep it simple.

Ensure it is well-formatted, free of errors, and branded to your company. The more sophisticated the branding, the more it will reinforce your brand and reflect well on you.

Slideshows are uploaded via LinkedIn's sister company SlideShare.net. The beauty of this is that Slide Share also attracts a high volume of traffic and ranks well in search engine results. When setting up your profile, be sure to complete all the information required and fill out the company description with a call to action and keywords. This will become another valuable source of lead generation for you.

In your slideshow, you can add a clickable button that links out to a webpage of your choice. You can set this within PowerPoint when creating the slides by adding a hyperlink. If you are using a free account on Slideshare it usually is after the 4th slide that you can have an active button or hyperlink. Things are always changing so do double check upon uploading to see if it does activate.

Keys to a good slideshow:

- Create a professional brand image using your logo and colour pallet well.

- Ensure photos are large, so they can be easily seen within the viewer.

- Convey your key points quickly and simply, with bullet points and as few words as possible.

- Ensure it is well-formatted with no typos.

- Include your contact information and a call to action.

- Use SlideShare.net to upload and ensure your account information also directs people to your business.

Slides

If you've got an event coming up or there is a particular offer you'd like to make, uploading a presentation with just a few slides is a great way to deliver your message. Again, it needs to get people's attention, so you'll want to be sure the first slide has a large font and minimal information, so it shows up well when sitting on your profile. More information can appear on the next slide once you have the person's attention but remember to check how the font size renders before publishing.

- Keep the slideshow short.
- Remove it after the date has passed.
- Create a simple first slide, so it presents well in the thumbnail on your profile.
- Ensure you brand it properly.
- Include all relevant information.

Infographic

Graphics always tend to get people's attention more than heavy text. If you can communicate statistics or a key message via a info graphic, this can get you a lot of attention. Info graphics are easy to share and tend to go viral.

You can use pre-existing research or do your research. Think about your target audience and likely presentations they might have to make to their colleagues and industry, about your topic. Consider designing a graphic they might use within their meetings to convey their point or might want to share with their network. The more informative it is, the better.

Always make sure to brand it well and put your key company information on as you never know when it might come back to you.

- Create something your audience can use to communicate to their audience, industry, and decision makers.
- Be prepared for a good info graphic to go viral by adding the right information about your company.
- Label correctly and link back to your key information, so it leads into your sales funnel.

Portfolio

For those who are artists, photographers, or designers, uploading portfolio items is a great way to demonstrate the quality of your work. There are various formats you can use to upload your portfolio that is visually appealing and user-friendly.

Ensure the portfolio is branded to you with all key links back to yourself and the original work where possible. Remember, we are in a social economy, so people look for social validation. They will want to see your work in action where possible. If your work has been used professionally and is featured on someone else's site, link to it. This will add to your credibility. A word of warning, however: Make sure that your work was the final version used as this can cause problems if your work ranks in the search engines for this product or project. Your client isn't going to be very pleased if your version is coming up in the search engine results when it wasn't used. When linking, it is worth asking your client first.

- Put your work into context by adding a short description that details the problem you solved for them by completing this work.
- Provide links to where the work can be found in its original form, i.e. so your client can gain something too.

- Check back with your client regularly to ensure it is the most up-to-date version.

Webinars

Webinars are great to feature, but poor to rely on. When using them, be clear on your reason for including and make sure you back them up with a mixture of other, shorter types of media.

Webinars do tend to be quite long with lengthy introductions, and for people who haven't yet opted to spend an hour with you listening from beginning to end, they won't listen beyond 30-seconds. Displaying them is fine for demonstrating you do webinars, but you might consider making a shorter video to act as a trailer for your webinar.

Again it is always about considering what someone is on the platform for. You can guarantee a person zooming around LinkedIn won't be in the right mind-set to opt in for a 40-minute webinar without having made a prior plan to do so.

- Don't rely on them. Use a mixture of media, so people have a choice on how to interact with you.

- Create a trailer for your webinar

- Make a slideshare with links to your library of valuable content, signposting your prospects to valuable content they may like making it easy for them to come back later.

- Edit the opening of the webinar to be completely on-point and delete any waffle to increase the chances of a person deciding spontaneously watch it.

Sample Chapters

If you've written a book, providing sample chapters is a great way to get people interested. You can take these straight from your manuscript and save them as a PDF with a call to action on the last page telling the person where they can buy it, ideally with an active link if you have the software to do so.

Again, remember that you only have so much of someone's attention, so you'll want to engage them quickly. You'll want to be sure what you upload remains within copyright, so be sure to add the symbol and 'All Rights Reserved.' The general publication text used to protect you in a book should also appear, but place it at the end of the file and after the call to action, rather than having it at the front of the sample as within a book. If your prospect has to click through this basic information, they might not continue.

Remember, the synopsis of the book and reviews are what usually entices a person to read a book. Be sure to include these as well, before the sample chapters, so someone can go through the normal buying process when considering a book.

The book will be a PDF version, and the first page will be the thumbnail that appears on your profile. Therefore, include a picture of the front page of the book as the first page of the document before formatting into PDF. This will ensure your colourful cover will be shown on your profile, grabbing people's attention.

Consider again how the book will show up in a LinkedIn viewer. It will probably be necessary to increase the text size dramatically to make it an easy read.

- Engage the reader from the outset by including the synopsis and reviews before the sample chapters, so they can sell themselves on spending time with the content.
- Include the front cover of the book in the main file, so it shows on your profile and re-enforces your brand.
- Add the link to where to purchase, at the end of the sample. Ideally using a hyperlink.
- End the sample halfway through a paragraph, so the reader wants more.
- Ensure the sample holds the appropriate copyright.

- Place legal items at the end of the book sample after the call to action. It needs to be there but will turn a prospect off if they have to work to scroll past this information.

Video

For creating content video, there are plenty of style options you could consider.

The video you upload can be as long as you like, though if you don't have an upgraded account on YouTube, you will be limited to 10 minutes. (Upgrading is simple. You just have to apply, providing your mobile phone number. After adding an activation code, you'll be able to upload longer videos.)

When crafting your video, there are a number of things to consider and challenges to weigh. When we decide to watch a video, our eyes usually go to the length of the video, and from there we consider whether the information we'll receive is worth the investment of that amount of time. A long video could put a person off watching. If someone is keen, they will at least start watching the video and tell themselves they can switch it off when they're ready.

The alternative is to create shorter well-labelled videos that stagger your information. The only problem is you can't control which of the short videos on your profile people will start with, even if you say 'start here.'

Thus, when creating your video, you'll want to ensure you start well, communicate your key information/objective, and avoid waffle. Ideally, you want to keep answering the questions your target market is asking in a succinct and structured way. At each stage, your viewer is going to be considering whether to continue watching. For those who aren't your target market, you'll want them to get the key information about you and move on. But for those who are your target market, you'll want to keep them right to the end, and this is why structuring your video to reveal more in-depth information as it progresses is important.

There are several types of videos you can produce—some can be done in isolation, and others can work as segments of a longer video.

The Pitch

This explains what you do and how you do it. A good pitch will start with one sentence that instantly lets someone know exactly what you do, and is followed with a sentence that says how you do it. Next, you want to tell people why you do what you do. The length will range from one to three minutes tops.

The Interview

Having started with a great opening to the video, you can add an interview where you discuss your approach to business and why someone should choose to work with you over someone else. You can have someone asking you questions (including the question at the beginning of your answer), post the questions up on the screen, or simply edit them together with one topic following another. The style is entirely your choice. Overlaying it with music will create an exciting/engaging feel to the video, and adding in extra pictures or videos as you're talking will be more visually stimulating while providing more insight.

Client Interviews

This video allows your clients to explain what you do and how well you do it in a spliced-up video, usually with some gripping music behind. It can be mixed with visuals of clients and staff in action delivering your service or product. It can feature interviews with you, the CEO, or the staff. These videos tend to leave people excited and intrigued.

How-To Videos

The official purpose of content marketing is to provide educational items that help your audience learn more about the subject or problem they need to solve. These videos will come with no agenda but to provide a service and add value. In them, you'll want to answer a popular issue the majority of your target audience will have and show them exactly how to fix it. To get value from it, ensure you include all of your contact details, but avoid any sales pitch.

It probably isn't a good idea to add these videos to your profile as there is no saying what problem a prospect wants to be answered, and thus you could overload them by supplying all answers. But like we said with people who product podcasts or content series, adding them gives a strong impression as to what you do and how someone might engage with you. You'll want to consider this one carefully before going ahead.

Publishing Articles

16

LinkedIn also provides the opportunity to publish lengthy articles direct onto the platform. This is a great idea since the articles will gain instant exposure to your network and sit on your LinkedIn profile.

The best types of articles to create are timely, thought-provoking ones that ignite a conversation. It goes without saying that the more likes, comments and shares you get, the more exposure your article achieves and more views your profile gets. The more controversial and opinionated (within reason of course) you are, the more you'll provoke a response.

As the articles do stay on your LinkedIn profile and show in date order, avoid adding content that is very narrow in nature and personal. For example, specific 'How-to' items that the majority of your audience won't be asking, or personal disclosures about something that happened to you and how you felt about it. This type of content is fine in a status update that is fleeting but not in fixed content that promises to add value simply by the length of it. It might be too early in the relationship for a prospect to learn this type of information about you. Consider too the context. Why are you saying it? Like all things we publish LinkedIn, always have your prospect front of mind – why are they reading this and what do they need to take away from it? Avoid self-centered conversation that adds no value to your prospect, as they won't like you for it.

Publishing content is a great way to get known as a Thought-Leader and expert within your industry.

Always make sure to finish the article with a call-to-action, either to advance through your sales funnel or by providing links to similar content, they might like.

While LinkedIn does provide your photo, name, and headline at the bottom of each article you publish, consider adding an 'About The Author' paragraph with clickable links. This way you take greater control over your message.

Measuring Results

The obvious result to measure, of course, is the number of new leads that come into your business and how well-educated they are about what you do. You should start to see that your first contact with your prospects is more advanced as they come more informed about what you do, with more specific questions relating to it. While you can put metrics in place to begin measuring this, a good amount of it will be subjective. You'll have to play it by ear.

If you opt for longer videos, beyond just a 30-second pitch, you will have some trouble measuring how many people watch it as YouTube doesn't count a video as having been viewed unless the majority of it has been watched. You can use YouTube analytics to see where people generally switch off. But don't be afraid of people switching off because this is just your target market disqualifying themselves as potential clients. It's those that watch to the end that are your ideal clients, and this is the statistic you want to pay attention to—though you won't be able to follow up since you don't have their information.

When people do call your office, it's a very good idea to ask them how they heard of you and what information they've engaged with. You'll probably find it is those who have watched your webinar or other videos and spent time with your content that is more open to having a buying conversation with you. If they didn't watch a video, they could still be in research mode or could be taking advantage of a special offer with no intention of buying.

For companies serious about measuring results, I suggest consulting with a social media agency that can provide full guidance as to how best to do this.

The
EXPERT
ECONOMY

Are you a serviced based business selling your time for money?

If so, join us at www.TheExpertEconomy.co.uk

In our fast-paced, busy lives, we really don't have time to waste when it comes to winning new clients and building our business.

What we need is for our name to come up in all the right conversations and our most ideal clients to come to us pre-sold and ready to buy.

Something that, with right marketing approach, is actually easy to achieve. All you need is a compelling call-to-action, clear packages and pricing, and a structured sales conversation.

If you would like help implementing these things into your business than join us. You might like to start reading my new book The Expert Economy: How to Build a Business Doing What You Love or jump right in and follow our 8-part online training course.

Either way, come find out more by visiting:
www.TheExpertEconomy.uk

About Us

Established in 2015 and based in the UK, TheProfile.Company supports solo entrepreneurs, small businesses, sales teams, recruiters and corporates all over the world to create engaging LinkedIn profiles that convert into paid business.

It was founded by Naomi Johnson, author of What to Put on Your LinkedIn Profile, Grassroots to Green Shoots, and The Expert Economy.

Having reviewed hundreds of LinkedIn profiles Naomi found that the majority of talented small business owners – experts within their field – where lacking vital business structures that, if put in place, would radically change their results.

Wanting to help clients tip the balance from spending 70% of their time searching for new clients to spending 70% of their time billing clients, Naomi created The Expert Economy; a published book and online course.

twitter.com/TheProfileCo

uk.LinkedIn.com/company/theprofile-company

www.TheProfile.Company

About the Author

Beginning her career working for several corporates, Naomi has completed a business degree, obtained Chartered Institute of Personnel and Development qualifications and run several companies. She is the author of three books: What to Put on Your LinkedIn Profile, Grassroots to Green Shoots and The Expert Economy.

Naomi ran the Rock Your Profile stand at LinkedIn's annual conference in 2013 and 2014, providing strategic consultation to many of the world's leading organisations.

In 2015 she began TheProfile.Company and spent three years writing LinkedIn profiles for business owners around the globe. In 2017 Naomi launched The Expert Economy determined to help talented business owners who sell their time for money tip the balance and spend more time billing clients than actually looking for business.

uk.LinkedIn.com/in/naomijohnsonuk

Other Books by Naomi Johnson

The Expert Economy

Published 2017 by
AchieveTODAY

ISBN: 978-0-9568055-6-0

The world we are living in is changing. With technology revolutionising how we live, our local markets have become global, barriers to entry in business have crumbled, and competition for skills has increased dramatically. Job contracts are now shorter and more people are becoming freelance or starting their own businesses.

Learning how to master our own career trajectory, build a personal brand and win business is now a basic requirement for many.

Speaking directly to small business owners and solo-entrepreneurs that sell their time for money, Naomi Johnson maps out a clear-cut strategy to build a business selling your expertise and doing what you love.

By implementing this teaching, you'll quickly position yourself as the 'go to' expert within your industry and have your name comes up in all the right conversations so prospects come to you pre-sold and ready to buy.

In this book you will learn how to:
- Create a compelling call-to-action that has your prospect eager to speak to you
- Cultivated a new marketplace where prospects only want to work with you
- Create attractive packages your prospects will want to buy that also meet your financial outcomes and fulfil you
- Script sales conversations so they feel natural and lead to the right outcome; whether that is to work with you or recommend you
- Craft content that speaks directly to your prospects at each stage of their buying journey
- Position yourself, so you no longer compete on price and you're the only person your prospect wants to work with.

Buy it now at
www.TheExpertEconomy.co.uk/Book

Grassroots to Green Shoots

Published 2010 by
AchieveTODAY

ISBN: 978-0-9568055-0-8

In this book, Naomi deals head-on with the 'get rich quick' industry and speaks frankly about what it really takes to be successful. She reveals the secret to making the transition from nine-to-five work to full-time entrepreneurship, finding extra money in your monthly budget to invest in your potential business, and working out whether your business model can really meet your financial targets and get you the life you want.

Drawing on the wisdom she has gained from her own mistakes, Naomi holds nothing back as she shares from her own journey and first-hand experience. By reading this book, you will avoid many of the unspoken pitfalls successful business gurus don't think to tell you—things that if left unchecked will mean 'game over' for you before you know it.

This book is perfect for small-business entrepreneurs who are starting to realise that the entrepreneurship revolution may not be quite as easy as the ride it's been billed as. If you are just starting a business, this book is a must-read.

Grassroots to Green Shoots is now available on Amazon.

Discover more about how to use LinkedIn to position yourself as the 'go to' expert within your business and build a thriving business.

Watch this in-depth webinar with free workbook.

Go to: www.TheExpectEconomy.co.uk/Webinar

www.ingramcontent.com/pod-product-compliance
Lightning Source LLC
Chambersburg PA
CBHW060528210326
41519CB00014B/3170